CHILDREN AND THE MARTIAL ARTS

An Aikido Point of View

CHILDREN AND THE MARTIAL ARTS

An Aikido Point of View

By Gaku Homma

Translated by Yutaka Kikuchi

North Atlantic Books
Berkeley, California

Domo Productions
Denver, Colorado

Published by
North Atlantic Books
P.O. Box 12327
Berkeley, California 94701

and

Domo Productions
988 Cherokee Street
Denver, Colorado 80204

Book design by Domo Productions
Cover design by Paula Morrison
Printed in the United States of America

Children and the Martial Arts: An Aikido Point of View is sponsored by the Society for the Study of Native Arts and Sciences, a nonprofit educational corporation whose goals are to develop an ecological and crosscultural perspective linking various scientific, social, and artistic fields; to nurture a holistic view of arts, sciences, humanities, and healing; and to publish and distribute literature on the relationship of mind, body, and nature.

The author and publisher of this instructional book are not responsible in any manner whatsoever for any injury which may occur by reading and/or following the instructions herein. It is essential that before following any of the activities described in this book, the reader should first consult a physician for advice on whether or not the reader should embark on the physical activity described herein. Because the physical activities described herein may be too sophisticated in nature, it is essential that a physician be consulted.

Library of Congress Cataloging-in-Publication Data

Homma, Gaku, 1950–
    Children and the martial arts: an aikido point of view / by Gaku Homma.
      p. cm.
    Includes index.
    ISBN 1–55643–139–2 : $16.95
    1. Aikido. 2. Self defense for children.
I. Title.
GV1114.35.H66   1993
613.7'148—DC20

93–2811
CIP

FOREWORD

The topics I have written about in this book have been on my mind for many years. I now feel relieved to have been able to share them.

Over the years, I have found that the children who come to my *dojo* are fortunate in many ways. Their greatest fortune is that their parents care about them. They get up early on weekend mornings and bring them to the *dojo* to practice. They help the little ones take off their jackets and shoes. They do many things to show their children that they want to help them.

I've seen many parents and children share special moments. Unfortunately, there are many children who don't enjoy loving relationships with their parents. This book will undoubtedly be read by parents who care very much about their children. It will probably make some people angry. It presents a different look at martial arts: a view that is more critical of violence than most people will expect. I also hope adult students take note of some of my points in this book. There is much to help them in their own studies, and teachings especially of children.

The most important task for my generation is to think of what we can do for our children and young people. We need to show them the leadership qualities we want them to inherit. I hope that this book will provide inspiration to other martial artists teaching children. I hope that it makes them think about their responsibility to children and provokes discussion about martial arts teaching and children. I hope that it makes other instructors put macho, violent images aside and consider the effect that martial art training has on the long-term development of children.

I would like to extend my heartfelt appreciation to Yutaka C. Kikuchi for translating my manuscript from its original Japanese into English, to Becky M. Kikuchi for typing and proofreading the manuscript, to John Cruise and Jeff Gregory for editing, to Emily Busch as project coordinator, and to Daniel Marion for creating the excellent illustrations.

Also, I want to thank the staff and members of Aikido Nippon Kan in Denver for giving me continuous opportunities to learn — the things I know now and the things I will come to know in the years ahead.

Gaku Homma
November 1992
Denver, Colorado

TRANSLATOR'S NOTE

In June of 1982, I joined the author of this book, Gaku Homma, in Denver, Colorado, and became involved in the activities of Nippon Kan. As is true in the founding period of many organizations, twenty-four hours did not seem enough to make a day. Our activities, while placing the main emphasis on Aikido training, varied from teaching Japanese cultural courses, such as *Sado* (tea ceremony), *Kado* (flower arrangement), offering Japanese cooking lessons, and giving demonstrations of things Japanese, like *Origami* (paper folded into a variety of shapes) and *Shodo* (brush calligraphy).

We were busy day in and day out, but that wasn't all we did. Because we didn't have any financial support from any public or private organization, we had to spend much of our spare time working to earn a living. I still remember days we weren't sure at all whether we could make enough money to buy food. Those were tough days. Aikido Nippon Kan *dojo* opened at its current location in 1983, and by the time I had to return to Japan at the end of 1986 for family reasons, the operation of the *dojo* had shifted from the founding period to a growth period. By then I had finished the translation of Homma Sensei's first book, *Aikido for Life.* In early March of 1991 I was asked if I was interested in doing the translation of this book.

At that time, Becky, my wife, and I were preparing for the arrival of our first child, and the title of the manuscript, "Children and the Martial Arts: An Aikido Point of View," struck me with great interest. Even before I finished reading the manuscript, I was sure that I would enjoy translating it. The children's class started when the *dojo* was still on Federal Boulevard in West Denver with only three or four students. I still remember back then waiting at the entrance of the *dojo* hoping that somebody would show up. It was a long time ago, it seems. It is hard to imagine from today's children's class the tentativeness we had when we started, and realize the fact that all those years resulted in this book.

In translating, I came across many occasions that helped me think through how I wanted to raise our child. Homma Sensei's memories of his childhood reminded me of my childhood, which

obviously was a great part of my personality forming period. When Homma Sensei analyzes how parents' expectations in martial art training reflect on their attitudes, led me to contemplate how I want to shape our children in our family. As an adult student of Aikido, many aspects of Homma Sensei's work described here apply to my training and life.

I tried my very best to communicate what Homma Sensei wanted to express in this book; I hope that readers will have a clear understanding of his views and intentions.

Yutaka Kikuchi
June 1992
Tokyo, Japan

TABLE OF CONTENTS

Continued

PART 1

MARTIAL ARTS TRAINING
AS AN EDUCATIONAL TOOL

INTRODUCTION

In the fifteen years that I have lived in Denver, I have been able to observe many facets of American culture while teaching the Japanese martial art of Aikido. I am the founder of Aikido Nippon Kan, the largest Aikido *dojo* (school) in the Rocky Mountain region. In addition to my responsibilities as chief instructor at Nippon Kan, I am still a student of the martial arts and I still train every day.

If all I did was teach Aikido, I would be at the same level I was fifteen years ago. A true martial artist seeks "the life of *Do* (the way or path)," which can be accomplished only by continuous training and constant growth. The concept of *Do* is, indeed, the essence of Japanese culture. *Do* is the path that has no end. This concept is also at the heart of many Japanese disciplines — Aikido, Karate-do, Kendo, Judo, *Kado* (flower arrangement), *Sado* (tea ceremony), *Shodo* (brush calligraphy), etc. To put it another way, true martial art training means a life-long commitment to learning. Therefore, if you are considering martial arts training for yourself or for your children, I believe you should examine the choices carefully before selecting a teacher or a *dojo*.

I have studied martial arts for more than thirty years, and for many of those years I have taught Aikido to children. This book is based on my personal experiences and from my experience teaching children's class at Nippon Kan. The opinions in this book do not necessarily apply to all Aikido *dojos*. There are many *dojos*, with many offering quality methods of education. For me to try to speak for all Aikido schools would not be fair to other schools or to readers. As you read, you might notice that Nippon Kan is mentioned frequently. Please understand that what I can speak best about, is what I know, which has resulted in Nippon Kan's teaching method. I would be interested to compare my experiences and ideas about martial arts training for children with those of others, but I haven't found many books on the subject.

I have often asked myself, "How can a person in my position — a fully "made-in-Japan" martial arts instructor who lives and teaches in the United States — provide the best possible method for teaching a traditional Japanese martial art to American children? I have tried to look at the situation from both a traditional

Japanese perspective and a contemporary American perspective, and I have spent countless hours searching for a way to blend the two points of view. This book is the result.

When your child approaches you and says, "Mom, Dad, I'd like to try martial arts training," you'll naturally want to find the best *dojo*. Before making a decision, you should look at the big picture and evaluate the possible influence and results of such training. Begin by asking yourself, "Is martial arts training really good for my child? Or for any children?"

I believe that martial arts training can be very good for children. It teaches skills that help children deal with everyday situations. But not all forms, teachers, and martial arts *dojos* are the same. How can parents make an intelligent decision? Get as much information as you can. (Please note that, throughout this book, when I refer to "parents" I am using the term broadly to include everyone who is involved with raising children.)

While this book will be particularly beneficial for those who teach Aikido to children, it also contains information of interest to adults — instructors and students alike. I hope that the views of one Japanese martial artist will give the reader insights into American and Japanese culture.

In this book I will look at martial arts training from many different angles. My hope is that it will help parents to ask intelligent questions before they choose a martial art for their child.

TAE-KEN-AIKI-JU-KA-NIN-DO

Those of you who are familiar with martial arts might know what tae-ken-aiki-ju-ka-nin-do is. Probably not. Before I explain it, I would like to tell you a story about the *dojo* where I teach Aikido.

Each fall the *dojo* receives about twenty telephone inquiries a day, more than any other season. Most of the calls go something like this:

"Our son/daughter just finished summer soccer, and we're thinking about putting him/her in a martial art school. What do you teach at your school?"

"We teach a Japanese martial art called Aikido."

"How is the Karate you teach different than Taekwondo?"

"We don't teach Karate. We teach Aikido. It is different from Karate and Taekwondo. Would you like me to send you some information about our school?"

"Is it like Ninja training? I used to practice Kempo. Is it like Kempo? Is it like Jujitsu?"

These calls can last up to twenty minutes. When the caller has run out of things to say and questions to ask, I usually finish by saying, "Why don't you bring your child to the *dojo* so you can see a class for yourself? If it interests you, we can talk some more." The caller still has no idea what Aikido is or how it's different than other martial arts.

Let's look at it another way. Let's say I sell apples. The caller wants to talk about peaches and melons. Finally, after twenty minutes, he decides that I sell grapes! It's impossible to describe apples to someone who doesn't know apples, and it's impossible to explain what my *dojo* offers over the phone to someone who doesn't know Aikido.

No matter what I say over the telephone, parents are surprised when they see their first Aikido class. As they watch the children practice, they can tell that this Japanese martial art training is not like the activities they are accustomed to. And although they don't know anything about Aikido, its background, or the effect it will have on their child, they sign up and hope it will bring out something special in their child. It surprises me that they make such an important decision so quickly.

When I first began teaching, I spoke to local teachers about the principles behind Japanese martial arts training. Afterward, one school teacher said, "Neither parents nor children take martial art training as seriously as you expect them to. If they don't do Aikido, there's always soccer, or baseball. If they don't work, then they'll try Taekwondo. Then maybe skiing." The other teachers agreed.

I realized that there is a great difference between the way martial arts are viewed in Japan and the way they are often viewed in the United States. In Japan, whether it is school education or instruction given in the home, martial arts training is a highly regarded teaching method. In the United States, most people think of it as simply one of many available recreational activities.

I think it is a dangerous mistake for a parent to let a child study a martial art unless the parent understands that martial arts training is a method of education. This book is about Aikido training as an educational tool. Even though Aikido has become popular around the world, there are many parents who confuse it with other martial arts.

Why do people expect a peach, a melon, or a grape when they're offered an apple? One reason is that there aren't any sources of information that explain the differences between Aikido and other martial arts. Another reason is that the martial arts have become big business. People see martial arts everywhere — in movies, cartoons, advertisements, etc. After seeing so many flashy portrayals of other martial arts, it's not surprising that they don't know what Aikido is.

This book isn't meant to be a step-by-step training manual for instructors, or The ABCs of Aikido. It's an explanation of Aikido as a method of education, and I hope that it gives instructors, parents and children something to think about — educating children through martial arts training.

It's also about martial arts in general. Remember Tae-ken-aiki-ju-ka-nin-do? No, it's not a strange Japanese incantation. It's more of a martial art fruit salad. What do you get when you mix Taekwondo, Kendo, Aikido, Judo, Karate, and Ninja? Tae-ken-aiki-ju-ka-nin-do. Tae-ken-aiki-ju-ka-nin-do is a mixed-up martial art concept. I would like to describe Aikido, the apple of our martial art fruit salad, and the similarities and differences between Aikido and other martial arts. Furthermore, I would like to explain the very important relationship between Aikido training and children.

AIKIDO: PLAYING AND LEARNING

Aikido comes from Japanese hand-to-hand-combat techniques that date back to the last half of the 16th century, an era of feudal war lords. During battles, warriors often broke or damaged their weapons, but still had to continue the fight. Hand-to-hand techniques evolved in this environment. The warriors developed ways to overcome enemies instantly using minimum force and effort. By mastering Aikido techniques, today's children can develop the ability to cope with the toughest of hardships, both physical and emotional.

Sounds pretty good, doesn't it? Even people who are familiar with Aikido would be impressed with such spectacular claims. But, if you know much about Aikido, you probably realize that the previous paragraph is not true. Someone who is not familiar with martial arts, however, might believe such a statement — about any martial art.

Let me try again to explain where Aikido came from. Aikido was founded in Japan by Morihei Ueshiba (1883-1969). His inspiration was to combine his knowledge of many different traditional Japanese martial arts with rigorous *Shinto* and Buddhist spiritual training. The result was Aikido. The founder believed that the root of martial arts is love. Therefore, the ultimate goal of martial art training is to arrive at harmony, and Aikido is a method of learning harmony. Since Aikido was first developed, it has spread steadily. Today, Aikido is practiced all over the world.

Many martial art schools make impressive claims about the results they get from their students, and many people believe them. After a person hears — and believes — such claims, the true story of Aikido's roots doesn't sound very impressive.

Some parents might read the first description of Aikido and think, "This is exactly what I'm looking for. A great way to educate my children." Parents who believe such sensational claims probably wouldn't be impressed by the real origin of Aikido. Other parents who find the first version a little too martial might be more impressed by the second version.

Each child that begins to study Aikido brings a unique background and a unique set of parents. However, I have found that many children and their parents share similar preconceptions about martial arts training.

Much of the information people receive about the martial arts comes from Hollywood. Martial arts heroes — young and old — are portrayed as winners; they become role models for children. It's not surprising that many beginners in the children's class come equipped with new martial arts uniforms and immediately try to use the techniques they've seen their heroes use.

Parents, too, expect certain results from martial art training, and often their desire to control their children extends into their children's martial arts classes. I often receive calls from concerned parents, searching for martial art training for their children, who ask: "Do you think my child would like Aikido? He's a very nervous kid. Would he fit in? He's kind of hyperactive. Do you think he would disrupt the class?" It's good that parents are concerned, but when class time comes around the children of such overprotective parents often cling to their parent's legs and are reluctant to take their first step onto the mat.

An Aikido class should be a place where children can develop their individuality within the context of martial arts training and without parental pressure. Of course, Aikido training involves certain rules that ensure safety, but above all, an Aikido class is a game for children to play.

In many years of teaching Aikido for children, I have seen hundreds of children. Regardless of their ages and backgrounds, I have found that once they're inside the *dojo* and participating in class, they all become — children. Children who run around the space, who jump all over, roll around, who get praised, who get scolded, who occasionally get into scuffles with other children, who make up, and again start running around. These are children at play. This play world is a true learning place for them because they learn best when engaging in their natural behaviors.

Using photos and illustrations it is possible to define what sorts of techniques and skills are used in Aikido. But the real value of Aikido training, I believe, is that it teaches students to deal with the kinds of situations they face in their everyday lives. I would rather not focus extensively on who the founder of Aikido was and the evolution of Aikido, but focus more on Aikido as a modern method of education. On the other hand, an understanding of Aikido's — or any martial art's — past can help us understand what it is today. Throughout this book I will present historical information when it helps explain the present state of martial arts.

TRADITION THAT WAS LEFT BEHIND

In the previous section I said that there is little reason for me to go into too much detail about the history of Aikido. However, I doubt that a martial art without roots, without a tradition behind it, can possibly have much value or relevance to everyday life. Ideally, a martial art should include traditions that are flexible enough to be adapted and made meaningful to today's society.

Each martial art has a unique background that defines it and distinguishes it from other martial arts. Just as there are many children currently participating in martial arts training, each with his or her own background, there are many martial arts — each with its own history and traditions.

It is possible to study and compare the characteristics of all the currently available martial arts. With such information, a person shopping for a martial arts *dojo* can determine which most closely matches his or her personal philosophy. Although it can become a very complicated process, it doesn't have to be.

Martial arts generally fall into one of three general categories:

1. "Fighting spirit." Martial arts in this category are characterized by straight forward attacks — kicks and punches. The responses to these attacks are also straight forward, usually with the intention of hurting or, if taken to the extreme, killing the attacker. Students learn to turn their bodies into deadly weapons. Tournaments are held; students are encouraged to participate. Winning is emphasized and rewarded. Many of the martial arts in this category have anti-authority roots.

2. "Unarmed combat." Martial arts that fall into this category practice mainly grasping, throwing and holding techniques; some utilize joint-manipulation techniques. Many of these martial arts date back hundreds of years to the Japanese *samurai* era, when *"kumiuchi"* techniques were developed and practiced. (*Kumiuchi* means unarmed combat.) Like the fighting spirit martial arts, unarmed combat martial arts often hold tournaments.

3. The third category of martial arts evolved from the sword-fighting techniques of *samurai* warriors. Sword techniques can be practiced alone, with a partner, or in a group. Tournaments are also common.

Where does Aikido fit within these groups? It doesn't.

There are no tournaments in Aikido, as the founder of the discipline, Morihei Ueshiba, specifically taught. Many strains of Aikido have evolved out of the original school, and today some hold tournaments. Mainstream Aikido *dojos* do not hold or encourage their students to participate in tournaments.

In children's Aikido classes, students practice in pairs, with both parties working together to perform a technique successfully. Students don't learn how to fight against each other; they learn how to cooperate with each other. This cooperative training philosophy doesn't develop or encourage a competitive attitude, so it's not surprising that children who practice Aikido don't compete in tournaments.

There are never any losers in Aikido. A child can't perform a technique successfully unless his or her partner is cooperative. This kind of cooperation isn't possible in win/lose situations. In Aikido, your partners are not your enemies; not your opponents. Your partners are the people who enable you to practice; who enable you to succeed. In Aikido practice, two partners face one another, close the distance, and make physical contact. Their forces join together and a technique is completed. The movements are rather soft and circular. Without partners, you can't practice Aikido. But few martial arts stress cooperation.

Over the last few years, a number of Hollywood films have popularized martial art heroes, and many new Aikido students have signed-up for beginner classes with preconceptions about martial arts.

In one series of movies, an aging Karate master trains a young student. The student learns his lessons well and in each movie he beats the bad kid in the final scene. The popularity of these movies led many parents to enroll their children in Karate classes. Many martial arts schools added "Karate" to their names with hopes of cashing in on the trend. Suddenly there were thousands of Karate schools. I remember feeling sorry for the true Karate instructors who had to watch as martial arts instructors of all sorts suddenly became "Karate" instructors.

One of Hollywood's contemporary martial arts heroes is often described in promotional material as a sixth-degree black belt in Aikido. His movies are typical Hollywood: lots of action, lots of fighting, and lots of bad guys getting beat up by a good guy who happens to use Aikido techniques. His popularity and the popularity of his movies have attracted many new Aikido students to my *dojo,* and probably to other Aikido *dojos.* Unfortunately, these people have been led to believe that Aikido is a violent form of self-defense that can be used to destroy an army of opponents. They forget that what they've seen is a movie; one shot over an extended period of time with stunt crews, special effects, and a great deal of editing. It is a portrayal with no basis in reality.

I have made it a rule to tell these people that if they chose to study Aikido because they were impressed by something they had seen in a movie, they chose the wrong martial art. If you are looking for a martial arts school for your child, I recommend that you try to look beneath the surface. Don't be too easily impressed by a Hollywood sales pitch.

Many martial arts schools try to attract new students by putting on flashy demonstrations. Teachers and students in colorful uniforms with colorful belts break boards or blocks of ice with spectacular punches and kicks. Schools push their students to attain increasingly higher levels, and there are frequent promotion tests. Parents at these *dojos* walk in and out of the practice area to watch their children in class, much like they would at a sporting event. Tournaments are held regularly, with as many different classes (by age, weight, and height) as possible. Shiny trophies are awarded: The emphasis is on winning and rewards.

The tremendous demand for martial arts training has enabled many people to operate successful martial arts *dojos.* But do the *dojos* that emphasize a competitive/combative approach and rely on belts and promotions offer the kind of training that will help students deal with the situations they face in their daily lives? I don't think so. These *dojos* are primarily profit-oriented businesses, and they adapt quickly as different styles come in and out of fashion.

It's very common these days for parents to buy uniforms for their children before enrolling them in martial arts classes. Unfortunately, not all children continue their martial arts training, and many uniforms end up gathering dust. I prefer giving new students and their parents an opportunity to sample Aikido before they invest in practice clothing. At Nippon Kan, students wear a simple, white uniform and a small patch. The uniform and patch are not required, or even encouraged, for beginners. We suggest that first-time students practice in a T-shirt and sweat pants.

Most good Aikido *dojos* do not feature competition, although children's classes do occasionally include training games (more on that later). Rather than hold — and charge for — regular promotional exams at Nippon Kan, we observe the development of each child from week to week, month to month, year to year. The children know that we keep an eye on everything they do in class; that we see them as individuals. Promotions are virtually automatic and are awarded on the length of time a child has been attending class. The number — and color — of belts is limited to give instructors a clear picture of the skill levels of the students. All students practice together: both older and younger; higher and lower rank.

Aikido has a long and respected tradition. In an age of flashy Hollywood martial arts heroes, good *dojos* try to preserve this tradition. A good martial arts *dojo* must offer much more than a colorful exterior. If you're thinking about enrolling your child in a a martial arts *dojo*, I suggest that you look for a stable, affordable school with a history of continuity and success.

IN THE TIME OF JOHN WAYNE

I have observed the influence of television and movies on martial arts with great interest. In the early '70s, Bruce Lee made Kung-fu famous. This fad was followed by Karate movies, then Ninja movies, and most recently Teenage Mutant Ninja Turtles.

When Bruce Lee was popular, children wore black Kung-fu shoes and played with rubber nunchaks. After that, when Karate became popular, uniforms changed from black to white. Children wore head bands with the Japanese characters for *"Kamikaze"* (divine wind) and *"Hissho"* (victory). When Rocky arrived, colorful boxer satins were "in." When the popularity shifted to Ninjas, who dressed from head to toe in black and dodged bullets while they chased bad guys, Ninja motorcycles and Ninja albums appeared. Newspapers contained stories about burglaries performed by Ninja-looking thieves. As each new movie was released, phones at martial arts *dojos* throughout the nation started ringing.

It was difficult for me, having studied traditional Japanese martial arts since I was eight years old, to watch as television shows and movies gave people a false view of martial arts. Unfortunately, some people still don't know the difference between true martial arts and those portrayed by Hollywood.

Let's take a look at an American "martial artist," John Wayne. The stories are often similar. A quiet, peaceful town is overrun by bad guys. A good guy wanders through town. He fights and beats the number one bad guy. There's usually a little romance. Many movies and television shows used this kind of theme. The fighting scenes from those shows and movies are quite different than the fights you see in movies today.

In old movies, fights were fair. The fighters honored a set of unwritten rules. Before fists start flying, the two men, or two groups of men, faced off while discarding their jackets and rolling up their sleeves. The fight begins with a punch; somebody falls. The fighter who threw the punch waits for his opponent to get up. His opponent wipes the blood from the corner of his mouth, jumps up, runs, and tries to tackle the guy who punched him. But the other guy is ready and counters the attack by pushing the attacker away with his foot. There are no kicks; kicks aren't allowed in the "Cowboy Code of Fighting." After exchanging a few punches, the fight turns into a wrestling match. The fighters roll around trying to choke and pin each other. The good guy manages to free one of his hands, punches the bad guy one last time, and wins the fight. The good guy walks away into the sunset; the loser is led away in humiliation by his fellow bad guys.

The fights in today's movies are much more violent than in the old cowboy movies, and each new movie seems to try and "outviolent" previous movies. I often ask the students at Nippon Kan, many of whom are in their thirties and forties, about the fights they got into during their childhoods. "They weren't like the fights kids get into today," they say. I suspect that when they were kids, their fights resembled the traditional cowboy fights in the movies.

In the old days, cowboy fights were like boxing matches. But today, cowboy movies use contemporary fighting scenes in an effort to compete with the skill level and intensity of the fights in martial art movies. Cowboys face off in martial arts stances, they punch like Karate experts and use a variety of jumping and spinning kicks. The fight isn't over until the bad guy is completely destroyed.

We have grown to expect this level of violence, even to enjoy it. Violence has become so commonplace that many people accept it without question. Many of these people also think that all martial arts *dojos* teach those flashy techniques, and they want to learn — or they want their children to learn — these techniques.

I believe that martial arts *dojos* should make their teaching philosophy clear. Those who own and operate martial arts *dojos* should realize that many people, misguided by television and movies, are searching for Hollywood-style martial arts. A good instructor should let parents know that traditional martial arts training is nothing like it is portrayed in movies and that such training can have a major impact on a child.

PUNCHING AND KICKING HIDE THE TRUE NATURE OF CHILDREN

One sunny afternoon, while I was at a park catching crayfish, a young boy rode up on his bicycle, parked it near me, and joined his friends playing nearby. Soon another boy, about the same age as the first one, walked by, picked up the bicycle, and looked around. When the first boy saw the second boy with his bicycle, he ran up and screamed, "That's my bike!"

"No, I found it here, so it's mine!" responded the second boy.

The two boys stood on opposite sides of the bicycle and began pulling on it. Suddenly, the first boy jumped aside, and took a "martial arts" stance. The second boy also jumped into a similar stance. They stared at each other.

They began to fight, and I decided to watch them a little longer. After an impressively long exchange of punches and kicks, they ran out of breath. Even though each boy threw a lot of punches and kicks, not many found their target. One boy seemed to have studied Karate; the other Kung-fu. Their techniques didn't match well, and, of course, the fight wasn't nearly as smooth as the fights you see in the movies.

Soon the struggle deteriorated into a wrestling match. One moment the first boy was on top, the next moment the second boy had the advantage. Finally, it was time for me to break up the fight. I walked up to the boys and pulled them apart. I told the second boy that his attempt to take the other boy's bicycle was wrong; that he shouldn't try it again. Then I said to both boys, "You guys are pretty tough. Where did you learn all the techniques you just demonstrated?"

They each said they studied a martial art. When I told the boys that I was a Japanese martial art instructor they both hurried away.

As I thought about the fight I had just witnessed, I realized the first part of the fight — the martial art style punching and kicking — were actions they had learned through their martial art training, and the second part — the grabbing and wrestling — were actions of instinct. The first part of the fight, in my view, was a mask that hid the boys' natural responses.

I have noticed the same kinds of behaviors in the students at my *dojo*. Children from six to fourteen years old share the same training space at Nippon Kan. At four or five years old is when children begin associating with groups of people other than their parents. The world becomes filled with playing with friends, dealing with new grown-ups, watching TV, reading through books; there is new information every day. Children who come to my *dojo* are influenced by the new world that has opened up around them.

Nearly all new students — adults as well as children — begin taking Aikido classes with preconceptions about martial arts. They believe that with a little practice, they'll be performing the same techniques they've seen their Hollywood heroes perform.

Children are constantly experiencing new things, but they don't yet have enough experience to evaluate all the new information. They're eager to try just about anything. The fighting boys first tried to use the martial art training they had learned, but it didn't work. They then reverted to their natural instincts, as though they had never studied martial arts — they instinctively grabbed and wrestled with each other.

What then are the natural actions of children? Why is it that a children's fight is usually grabbing and wrestling rather than punching and kicking? Because most children begin receiving martial arts training as soon as they are born. Infants quickly learn that mother's face must be grabbed gently. Punching-like movements are discouraged. Children learn that they must not "hurt" toy animals or dolls. As for kicking, children use their legs primarily for balance, which means that kicking is not a natural movement for them.

When children become old enough to play with other children, their parents teach them to be nice. Most parents want their children to be accepted and liked by other children; they don't want to raise social misfits. Even if a parent is a martial artist themselves they do not encourage young children to act aggressively, to hit or kick their playmates. In other words abrupt physical contact such as punching, kicking, and scratching is discouraged during early childhood. But, on the other hand, parents want their children to be active, running around the yard with friends, throwing balls, and wrestling with the neighbor kids. (Major complaints focus on dirty clothes!) When children frolic, like puppies, parents do not complain. I believe that these basic "techniques" that children learn at an early age — how to get along with each other — should continue to be developed in martial art training.

"Truce, not aggression. Harmony, not confrontation." These are basic principles of Aikido. Children who study Aikido learn that harmony is preferable to confrontation, that peaceful solutions are preferable to non-peaceful solutions.

When I think of how much energy parents spend teaching their children how to be nice to their brothers, sisters, and other children, I find it strange that many parents decide to enroll their five- and six-year-olds in martial arts classes that teach them how to punch and kick other children. What kind of message are we sending to the children who win trophies at martial arts tournaments? That a winner is the person who can outpunch and out-kick the opponent? That conflicts are best resolved by beating up your adversaries?

I mentioned earlier that there is no competition in Aikido; only classes. Children learn to perform techniques within a general set of rules. Every child who studies Aikido has a unique personality, and Aikido is not guaranteed to make every child happy. But it certainly nourishes a positive attitude, and it helps develop children who can live in harmony with other children. I don't know if the same thing can be said of all martial art *dojos*. As an instructor of a martial art, I sometimes question why children should study martial arts which teach aggressive techniques and promote competition.

I believe that a certain gentleness of spirit is part of the ethical foundation of the United States. Because I am first a concerned citizen, second a martial arts instructor, I am concerned about the kind of people that kids will grow into. We'll look more closely at this issue in the following sections.

CIRCULAR AND STRAIGHT MOVEMENTS

Imagine two rocks: one is from a river shore — smooth and rounded; the other is from a mountain peak — rough, jagged. The contrast of these two rocks goes beyond their outward appearance. The smooth stone seems warm and kind; the jagged stone seems cold and tense. Most people feel more comfortable around smooth, round objects than around rough, jagged ones.

I think that our attraction to smooth, round objects is the result of lessons learned at a very early age — a time when our world was full of soft, round things. A new-born baby's first sight is of its mother's face. Reaching out, the first things a baby touches are warm, soft, and round — mother's face and breasts. A baby's world is full of stuffed animals, soft blankets, and fluffy pillows.

Soon, reaching and touching are followed by rolling movements — from stomach to back; back to stomach. Crawling is next; then sitting up. And just as a baby's body is soft and round, so are its movements — even when sitting. Standing is quickly followed by walking. Before long the baby is a child, running, jumping, and spinning.

For about the first two years, children's movements are mostly circular, uninhibited, and directed towards reaching for a greater degree of freedom. Like a flower blooming, a baby's actions are all outward, opening. Before the age of two, an infant doesn't know how to be aggressive. Crying is the only defense. When older siblings tease or play too rough with younger children, parents remind them that babies require gentleness. For most children this is a first lesson in harmony and discouraging confrontation.

When children become old enough to join martial art *dojos*, they start to wear stiff uniforms and make straight line movements — punches and kicks — following the instructor's count. They learn jerky, start-and-stop techniques that look as if they're being shown on a slide projector, and they learn that the objective of a technique is to defeat an opponent. What kind of effect can this have on their attitudes and behavior?

Some *dojos* don't stress competitiveness during classes, but still encourage their students to participate in tournaments. The purpose of a tournament is to determine "winners." Trophies are awarded only to winners. And while everybody wants to be a winner, there are seldom as many winners as losers. Why would a parent encourage a child to participate in a martial arts tournament knowing that most of the children in the tournament will wind up as losers? Some martial art schools claim that training in preparation for tournaments builds "self discipline," "a challenging spirit," and "self control." But tournaments also create winners and losers, and no child wants to be a loser. Why put children in a position where many will lose?

Many martial arts tournaments also have *"kata"* competitions and demonstrations. A *kata* is a series of martial art movements — attack and defense — done alone. Many children perform *katas*, often at full speed and strength, as if fighting imaginary opponents. With each punch and kick there is a crisp sound of impact, created by an elbow or a knee slapping against the inside of the uniform. To create this Hollywood sound effect, the children stop their punches and kicks suddenly by locking their joints.

Some children use tricks to produce the sound of impact, such as by hitting themselves in the chest with their non-punching fist. A friend of mine who owns a martial art supply store recently commented to me that he hadn't been selling uniforms made of thin material lately because it didn't produce the desired sound effects. It bothers me to think of children's fragile joints being subjected to such jerky, unnatural motions.

In Japan, *"Budo,"* the path of the martial arts, means endless training of body and mind. The goal is to treat our bodies with the utmost care. A body that is in good condition can perform when called upon. From that point of view, damaging our own bodies is the worst possible thing we could do and defies the teaching of *Budo*.

Children aren't the only ones who should be careful about injuring themselves through martial arts practice. A few years ago, a Karate school in Florida invited me to be a guest instructor. As I was talking to one of the senior students, I noticed that he constantly swayed his head and rolled his eyes. I learned later that he got that way after many weeks of practicing breaking bricks with his head! Another student proudly told me that he had broken both of his shin bones while training. The accident occurred when he tried to kick his way through some baseball bats!

Although there are high ranking instructors of Karate in the United States who maintain traditional teaching methods, students sometimes believe that they can attain new levels of self-awareness by harming their bodies. Indeed, it might be impressive to see a person break bricks with his head and baseball bats with his shins, but is it worth the risk? Hearing such stories, I can't help but wonder about why some people practice martial arts. I also worry about what happens when imitative children see adults practicing such things. Although there may have been periods in Japan's history with this kind of focus, this self-abuse is far removed from the traditional philosophy of martial art practice.

GLORIFYING THE DENIAL OF LIFE

Before the concept of *Budo* became widely accepted, martial arts in Japan were commonly known as *Bujutsu*, which means "fighting skills" or "fighting techniques." The concept of *Do* (the "way" or "path") had not yet become associated with martial arts training.

If you study the history of Japanese martial arts, you'll find that different classes of people practiced different styles of martial arts. If we examine the weapons the various classes used, we can understand a little about the philosophy behind their development.

During Japan's Edo period (1603-1867), the population was divided into four different classes: *shi* (warriors), *noh* (farmers), *koh* (craftsmen), and *sho* (merchants). Only the warrior class, known commonly as *samurai,* were permitted by the *Shogun* (military overlord of feudal Japan) government to carry weapons, mostly long and short swords. The *samurai* class grew powerful during this period, and they often attempted to confiscate all weapons from the non-*samurai* classes.

People from the non-*samurai* classes who opposed the repressions of the reigning government were forced to use their hands and work tools as weapons. *Nunchaks* were originally used to shell rice grains; *tong-fa* were used to peel skin off of beans; *kama* (sickles) were for cutting grass, and a *sai* was originally the working end of a two-pronged pitchfork without the shaft attached. Obviously these are not traditional weapons, like swords, spears, bows, and flintlock muskets. You can see how the social structure of the Edo period influenced the martial arts that were practiced, and it's no surprise that the weapons and techniques developed by the non-*samurai* classes were very different than the martial arts developed by the *samurai.*

After centuries of practice and refinement, the *samurai* elevated *Bujutsu* (fighting skills) up to *Budo* (the way of martial arts), but still such practice was not permitted outside of the *samurai* class. Any member of a non-*samurai* class found doing so faced summary execution.

The people who chose to defend themselves from the ruling class risked their lives, and because defeat meant death, it's not surprising that they turned their bodies into lethal weapons. They developed great physical and mental strength, and they feared neither injury nor death.

Their very lives depended on their destructive power. To develop strength and mental toughness, these martial artists punched rocks, kicked through boards, and broke bricks with their heads. The next time you see a martial art demonstration featuring such techniques, remember the circumstances under which they began and ask yourself: What do these demonstrations have to do with today's world? There is a fundamental difference between martial arts which were developed to fight against authorities for political, religious, or ethical reasons, and those which were developed by the ruling *samurai* class. Although resistance-style martial arts have a long history, I believe they can have a negative influence on life as we now live it.

Most citizens of the United States are living in a time of relative peace. People are learning how to live with each other in harmony; to share mutual goals; to develop a healthy society. We don't have to turn our bodies into fighting machines. What we need is to return to our "round" selves; to learn how to take care of our bodies.

The Chinese character for *"bu"* (of *Budo*), means "to stop the spear" or "to stop fighting." Respect for life is the heart of *"Budo."* With this concept in mind, I think you can understand why there are no tournaments in Aikido. Although the mind ultimately controls the body, it is also true that repeated physical movements can influence the mind, forcing mental patterns to resemble physical actions.

Children can be taught to be combative. Military training facilities are a good example. Parents are often surprised at the quick changes they see in a child who has been sent to train for the military. It doesn't take much training to condition a child to march in step, to respond aggressively to an attack, or to pursue a goal without letting anything get in the way. Such training has great and permanent impact. How many times have you watched the nightly news and seen children in war-torn countries holding rifles, shooting the enemy? These children were taught by adults that killing their enemies is the right thing to do; the children do as they are told without question.

A child's mind is like a sponge, absorbing everything. Teaching children what's right and what's wrong should begin by teaching them it is better to get along with other people than to fight. In many martial arts classes for children, the teacher barks out a cadence while the children perform mechanical, rehearsed movements. The idea behind this approach is that when confronted by an opponent, the child will automatically respond with aggressive techniques that will disable the attacker.

I think martial arts that emphasizes straight-line (punch/kick), aggressive movements can have a long term effect on children that is more negative than positive. Aikido, on the other hand, is based on the natural roundness I spoke of earlier; a roundness that children learn from the day they are born. During Aikido class, children learn to work in harmony with their partners by meeting their oncoming force with smooth, circular movements. There is no punching and kicking; no sense of competition.

When children are unhappy their actions reflect their mood: they punch and kick things. When they are happy, they spin and roll and laugh. Children who practice Aikido quickly learn that they don't have to worry about winning and losing; that they are not under pressure to "beat" their partners. Free of the burden of competition, the children are free to enjoy themselves. As guides for our children, we hope to see them grow up with positive capabilities and temperaments. If this is true, I believe we have a responsibility to provide them with environments that encourage cooperative behaviors that will help them in life.

So far, we've looked at the history and philosophy behind the martial arts. In the following chapters, I would like to share some of the experiences I've had teaching Aikido to children.

SHOPPING FOR A MARTIAL ART OVER THE PHONE

What kind of shopper are you?

When I opened my Aikido *dojo* fifteen years ago, I was not exactly comfortable with English. I'm still not completely at ease with the language, but at least I understand the difference between bear foot and barefoot. Anyway, phone calls used to terrify me, especially those from people I didn't know. Naturally, many people called to inquire about classes and assumed that I could understand them. I learned to listen for certain key words, and before long I was able to understand the gist of a call even if I couldn't understand every word.

This talent reminded me of a student of mine who, although she could not read Japanese written languages, had learned to recognize two *hiragana* characters. She was able to find these two characters in text faster than any native reader. The reason for this, I discovered, was that because each character holds meaning for native readers, they read them all. Because only two characters had any meaning for my student, she could spot them quickly. My limited grasp of the English language left me in much the same situation.

I soon realized that many of the calls were similar. Eventually, I could predict the course of a call after only a question or two.

Here are a few examples:

"This is Nippon Kan. Can I help you?"

"Yes. I have a six-year-old son. I'm thinking about enrolling him in a martial arts class, and I've checked around." The caller then talks at length about the information he's gathered about other martial arts. "Karate isn't right," he says, and then mentions two or three problems he's found in his research. "Neither is Taekwondo." More reasons. This caller will often mention Aikido and the shortcomings he believes it has.

There's not much I can say to callers like this. They're not really asking questions; they're not interested in learning anything. They're simply trying to get the person on the other end of the phone to agree with them. Usually, these callers don't choose Aikido for their children. There's not much I can say that will change the conclusions they have already reached.

"This is Nippon Kan. Can I help you?"

"Well, I hope so. My daughter has no concentration. She never finishes the things she starts. Other kids pick on her, and she's scared of them. I was hoping that maybe martial art training would solve her problems."

"Does your daughter have any physical problems?"

"No. She's perfectly healthy."

"Then she has a lot going for her. What would you like me to do?"

"Well, I'd like you to help her improve her concentration. I want her to be a bit stronger, and not get picked on all the time."

"Are you familiar with Aikido, or any martial arts?"

"No, but from what I've heard, this kind of training is good for children."

This kind of caller has preconceptions about what a martial art will do for a child and assumes that all martial arts are basically the same. It's difficult to make such callers understand that taking a martial arts class will not solve all of a child's problems overnight.

The abilities to concentrate, to react in a positive way to adversity, and to reach goals, are developed over a lifetime. Some parents who find fault with their children hope that martial art training can be a quick fix.

I can't blame parents for thinking that martial art training can change their children overnight. A number of Hollywood productions have featured children who undergo miraculous transformations as a result of martial art training. All parents have dreams for their kids, perhaps even secretly hoping that they will turn into some kind of superhero, but it's not that easy. No martial art classes can make up for deficiencies in a child's early training. Parents are a child's most important teachers; children behave the way their parents teach them to behave. In Japan, there is a proverb that goes, "Children are a mirror of their parents, and parents are a mirror of their children."

I usually find that the children of such hopeful parents do just fine in Aikido classes. If they have shortcomings, they're not evident during class. They behave like the rest of the children.

Many calls don't last very long:

"This is Nippon Kan. Can I help you?"

"How much?"

"How much what?"

"Class fees. How much are class fees? And a black belt? How long?"

"That depends on the size of your child's waist."

Click.

"This is Nippon Kan. Can I help you?"

"My kid was hit in school. He needs some kind of self defense."

"Did you contact the school authorities? They can handle this kind of thing, can't they?"

"They wouldn't do a thing."

"If your child learns a martial art and hits back, the other kid may come back with a knife. Then what?"

Click.

Some parents who call are courteous and confident about what they are looking for:

"This is Nippon Kan. Can I help you?"

"My child is interested in Aikido training. Could you tell us a little bit about Aikido and your *dojo*? If possible, we would like to visit the *dojo* and see a class for ourselves."

"Sure. I'll mail you a pamphlet about our *dojo*. If you and your child are interested in watching a class, you are welcome to visit. After you've had a chance to see a class, you can decide if Aikido is what you're looking for. "

"That sounds good. We'll come for a visit."

Things often go very smoothly for callers like this, and their children tend to become good students.

Telephone calls are often the first contact parents have with me and my Aikido *dojo*. It is also my first introduction to their children. I'm afraid that during that first call, many parents find me opinionated and difficult to talk to. Many parents who call don't enroll their children. And that's a good thing. True, every parent who calls is a potential client, but I also need to be selective about the children who join up. It would be very easy for one child to hurt another during class.

As I said before, children are a reflection of their parents. Some parents look for a martial arts *dojo* that emphasizes aggressive techniques because they believe that these techniques are acceptable, even desirable. Some parents expect a martial art *dojo* to turn their children into superheros overnight. These parents aren't happy with anything less. I would rather discourage such parents during that first contact call than have them to enroll their children in a class that won't live up to their expectations.

When an infant first learns to stand up, it will stretch out its arms and reach for its parents. This is a very special moment. A parent must be careful not to let the child fall and get injured, but the child must have enough room to move and develop. Some falls are inevitable; that's how children learn to walk. Parents who want their children to study a martial art must give them the same freedom they gave them when they first learned to walk.

When children begin Aikido training, it is very important that they be free from the expectations of their parents. Parents must be willing to give their children the freedom to be themselves during class. When a parent calls and makes it clear that they want to control their child's training, I don't try very hard to sell them on Aikido.

I am not a businessman, I am a martial artist. I did not open my *dojo* to sell contracts, belts, and uniforms. Parents who call because they are concerned about the well being and development of their children deserve respect. My door is always open to parents and their children who wish to listen to my ideas and advice. I can only hope for patience on their part in trying to discover the direction in my methods.

THE WATER I GREW UP IN

I would like to tell you a bit about my childhood and the "the water I grew up in." I hope that by telling you a little about my early years, especially my early martial art training, you will be better able to understand my ideas about martial art training for children.

I spent the first twenty eight years of my life in Japan drinking Japanese water. Therefore, my perspective is fundamentally Japanese. Of course, more than fifteen years in the United States has changed me a great deal, but it doesn't mean that I've forgotten what I learned during my years in Japan. I have been exposed to very different, dynamic cultures. I have visited Japan many times in the last fifteen years, and have noticed changes in Japanese society and its people that I would not have noticed had I been living there all along. I am aware of the changes only because I have not been affected by them.

Having lived in two such different cultures, I evaluate things from two different angles. When I find myself in a new situation, I analyze it first from a Japanese perspective, then from my recently acquired American perspective. And back and forth. My ideas about martial arts are a combination of these two perspectives.

Americans may find it difficult to understand the Japanese perspective I bring to the martial arts; Japanese people may not comprehend the American perspective that I have added to Aikido — a traditional Japanese martial art. But I believe it is only natural that the ideas of a Japanese-born martial arts instructor, living in the United States and teaching American students, be a blend of the two cultures.

I'm over forty years old now; my childhood was a long time ago. Not only have many years passed, but the rate of change has been incredibly rapid. The Japan of today is much different than the Japan I knew as a child thirty years ago. But it was then that I learned how to play with other children, and when I began to learn some of the traditions that are at the heart of Aikido.

I was born into a well-respected family with deep historical roots. However, the years following WWII were filled with hardship for my family and our standard of living, although adequate, was by no means luxurious. As a young boy, I did not receive any special martial arts education not normally available to children my age at the time.

My martial art training officially began during the spring of 1958 when I started second grade. During the previous winter, I had followed some older students to a martial arts class and became interested. Back then, it was common for teachers with martial arts experience to teach martial art classes after school. I confess, I don't remember my very first class. But my father kept a diary at the time, and it contains references to my interest in martial arts.

What I remember most about this period was the time I spent playing with my friends. I was born at the peak of the baby boom that followed the war, so there were many young children in my neighborhood. It was easy to get a group of twenty to thirty children together to play. For the most part, our parents worked into the evening, so we played unsupervised until dark.

I remember how excited I was during my thirty-minute walk home after school. I would think about my friends and the things we would do as soon as I got home. My mother was always waiting for me with five *yen* in her hand for an afternoon snack.

As soon as I had the money in my hand, I was on my way out to play. I listened for the sound of the other kid's voices and headed in whatever direction I heard them playing. Every day, I spent my after-school hours outdoors playing with the kids in my neighborhood.

On one level, we played simply because it was fun. On another level — one I wasn't aware of then — the time we spent together was a learning experience for all of us. The games my friends and I played, the situations we experienced, were the same games and situations that all Japanese children our age experienced, especially for those of us who lived in the country.

When children play in a group, they learn what the rules are and why they must be followed. One of the first rules I learned was that the oldest children in the group were the leaders. In any group, small or large, there are leaders who organize the group's activities and set the example for the younger members. Among my playmates, the leaders were the children ages eleven or twelve. When children became teenagers and started junior high school, they developed a whole new set of interests and activities and no longer served as leaders of childrens' play groups. After three years of junior high school, they were considered grown-up — though they were not legally adults. They were given many responsibilities in the community and were expected to behave like grown-ups. Most of our group leaders were sixth graders. They would replace the former leaders who had moved on to junior high school.

Boys formed one group; the girls another. Boys and girls played in different places — the girls tending to play indoors. (At that time traditional family structure, as well as Japanese society, enforced strict gender-based codes of behavior. Boys were taught not to cry, to behave with control, and to carry out responsibilities. Girls were taught not to fight with boys, and were expected to be kind, soft spoken, and obedient.) For both groups — boys and girls — seniority determined the leaders, and everyone adhered to this unwritten rule. The oldest children were the leaders, and the youngest children followed their example, no matter how active, aggressive, or big the younger children were. If there was more than one child in the oldest age group, then the most authoritative got to make the calls. And because the idea of seniority is ingrained in Japanese people, our group leaders were not only respected by the younger children, they were also trusted by the parents of the younger children.

Respect for elders is at the heart of Japanese culture. Traditionally, the oldest son in a Japanese family is expected to act as a deputy to his father and is trained for this responsibility. The oldest child also holds a position of authority over the younger children.

Unlike in Western cultures, Japanese siblings do not call one another by their first names. Older children are allowed to use any name they want to address their younger brothers and sisters, but the younger children must address their older siblings as *"niisan"* (for an older brother) and *"neesan"* (for an older sister). (When it comes to children addressing adults, it is unheard of in Japan for a child to use a first name.)

My association with the other boys in my neighborhood was my first exposure to society outside of my family. Of course, by the time we were old enough to join a group, we were already familiar with the concept of respect for elders. This basic idea applied to our school life, to martial art practice, to brush calligraphy lessons, to everything. This tradition is part of what I call "the water I grew up in."

Our annual spring tree house project is good example of how the oldest children would lead the group's activities. Each spring, when the countryside turned green and everything was new and fresh, we would go into the mountains to celebrate our release from the long winter. The first thing we would do was build a tree house, which I've found is something that children all over the world do.

When we built tree houses, the oldest boys led while the younger boys learned from them. The leader would say something like, "We need a saw. You, go get it from your house." The boy who received the order was responsible for getting a saw — even, perhaps, if it meant being punished by his parents for "borrowing" from the tool box. Following the instructions of the oldest boys, the rest of us would move around on the mountainside gathering the materials we needed.

After the tree house was built, we of course needed weapons to protect our property from other groups. First, we created wooden swords from appropriately sized branches. The process was simple: Simply peel the bark off a small branch; leave a few inches of bark on one end for the handle, and you have a wooden sword! I remember wondering how our leader made his sword so quickly.

Next, we cut pieces from bamboo trees and made bows. For arrows, we collected small, straight branches. For arrowheads, we used soft bamboo grass. We made piles of small stones to hurl at invading groups. We used forked branches to create slingshots, which were highly prized because of the scarcity of rubber and elastic. When all of the weapons were ready, we took them up to the tree house.

We practiced their use and improved their designs. We divided into two groups — attackers and defenders — and held "scrimmages." The attackers tried to gain control of the tree house and the defenders, of course, tried to defend it.

All of this may sound dangerous, but there were few injuries because it was a rule to aim only at the legs. Sometimes someone would get bumped and start crying, but in most cases the boys who cried weren't really hurt. Unless an injury was serious in the eyes of one of the leaders, the battle continued. For the most part, little sympathy was given to anyone who started crying. However, if the crying was genuine and caused by an excessive use of force by another boy, the aggressor was punished. Sometimes an offender was sent home and was unable to return until he was pardoned by the leader.

No matter how rough things got, punching and kicking were taboo. Any boy caught punching or kicking was in for a severe scolding by his parents. A boy guilty of punching or kicking someone was often dragged by his parents to the house of the victim and forced to apologize. There was a clear line between what was and wasn't acceptable. Often, when parents got involved after someone got punched or kicked, the fun would come to a sudden end. That's why one of the strongest rules was: "We'll all get punished if somebody gets hurt. Don't hurt anybody!"

All of this may sound like a TV documentary about a primitive tribe in the Amazon. Our "tribal" activities were taught by the group's senior leaders to the group's younger members, who would eventually become leaders themselves. This tradition had been passed on year after year, for many generations.

The first things that boys would learn outside of their houses was how to build a tree house, how to make fake weapons, etc. In other words, how to do things as a group. I think that children around the world develop similar army-like activities.

The years after World War II were difficult for children in Japan. Money was scarce and parents couldn't afford toys. But by combining our imagination with a little creativity, we turned simple things — nails, tin cans, and fallen branches — into toys and games; the countryside was our playing field. Because we had few toys, our friends and our group were important, and we looked to our leaders for guidance.

When I think about today's youth gangs and the problems they are causing in many cities, I can't but help thinking that many of these children missed out on something during their early childhood and that their violent actions are an attempt to fill in what they missed. It is time for this generation of adults to look back and determine what we did to create a generation of troubled youths. In addition to their violence, today's street gangs today are known for their unity, their ability to act quickly, their group-oriented awareness, their loyalty — many of the same qualities cultivated by the groups I belonged to as a youth. I wonder, why is it that so many teenagers today join groups to learn things that children of earlier generations learned when they were much younger? It's an interesting thought.

Let me continue with my childhood story. We played nearly every day, whether it was warm or cold, sunny or cloudy. We played when it was dry and when it rained and snowed. We were very creative when it came to creating games. In summer, of course, we went swimming every day — some days our group leader would take us to the school swimming pool, other days to a nearby pond. He also taught us how to swim. Our parents and teachers trusted him with these responsibilities. As long as the leader was there to keep things under control, we were allowed to do a lot of things. When we wanted to go somewhere that required permission, all we had to do was to mention to our parents that we were going with the leader.

I can still remember the games we played and the things we did together. In autumn, we went into the mountains and picked nuts —as many as we could. We'd store them in a shack in the woods to share later. When winter arrived, we built a snow house called a *"kamakura"* and played inside. To build a *kamakura*, we piled snow into a big mound and then dug a hole in the middle. The snow house we created was big enough to hold ten of us. We made sleds and bamboo skis, and played outside until our pants cuffs were frozen solid. We chewed off the iceballs that formed on our wool gloves. We had games for all kinds of weather in every season. We didn't have many toys and we didn't watch TV, but everybody had many friends to play with. Later, I'll tell you a little bit about some of the games we played — some of which I still use for children's Aikido classes.

In recent years, the number of children in Japan has been decreasing. At the same time, the number of playgrounds has diminished, particularly natural ones. Add to that the growth of cities, crime, traffic, and increased academic pressure. Today, many Japanese children are sent to preparatory schools after they finish regular school to cram for college entrance exams. When you add all of these things together, it's easy to see why Japanese youths have so many more problems today than they did a generation ago — they never have a chance to be children.

You can see the problem in the increasing rate of suicides, mental illness, juvenile crime, street gangs, etc. A few years ago, Japanese educators and intellectuals were confident that the introduction of Western-style schools and teaching methods would help Japan. There's no doubt that the new methods produced more skilled and knowledgeable students, but they also produced a greater number of misfits, drop-outs, and unhappy youths. When I was young, a suicide or a case of mental illness was very rare and made big headlines. Not any more. The water I grew up in has changed. Sometimes it doesn't seem Japanese to me.

FORGET JUDO!

As I mentioned in the previous section, I grew up in a group and spent most of my free time with the other children. When I became old enough to become a member of my neighborhood group, I discovered that the oldest children were in Judo school. The younger members admired these group leaders, and followed them everywhere, like puppies. If the older boys crossed a road, so did the younger children. If the older children carried sticks, we found slightly shorter sticks to carry. I wanted to be the same as the older boys and do the same things they did. That's why I started going to Judo — classes were an excuse to be with the older boys.

My very first encounters with martial arts occurred before I entered school. In front of the house in which I was born there were 112 stone stairs that led to *Satake* Castle's *honmaru* (the main residential chambers in the castle of the warlord who governed the region). I was born within the perimeter of the castle, which was built during the *Edo* period (1603-1867), and grew up in its shadow, finding many interesting spots to play.

I remember watching students from the nearby high school as they walked to martial arts practice each day during their annual training camp. There were students from Judo and Kendo clubs, easily distinguished by the uniforms they wore. They practiced without shoes, beginning each training session by climbing the stairs. First they would run up the stairs a few times, shouting *"Essa-hoisa! Essa-hoisa!"* Then they hopped up like rabbits. After that, they made pairs and carried each other up and down. They held onto their partner's ankles, and wheelbarrowed up. I often heard their coaches striking the students with their bamboo swords.

I watched them from the second floor of our house, and I remember being very impressed. Because I watched them every day, they began to notice me. Eventually, I became their mascot. When they were in *Gasshuku* (seasonal training camp) they practiced from 6 o'clock in the morning until 10 o'clock at night and slept in the school on *futons* (bedding cushions filled with cotton) they brought from home. The camp lasted about a week. At the time I had no idea how difficult their training was; I'm sure it was difficult.

Back then, and still today, the boys' high school had at least one *dojo.* In many cases Judo and Kendo clubs shared one practice space. One step inside the *dojo*, and you were hit by the smell of sweat, old uniforms, and *tatami* mats. You could recognize a Kendo *dojo* blindfolded by the smell of indigo dye. I still can remember the smells vividly.

My early encounters were not limited to my stints as a mascot; I remember another incident. My family lived near a university, and for a time we shared our home with a couple of students. They often practiced using *nung-chuks* and *sai.* I don't recall the style they practiced; just that they were members of a Karate club at the university. Later, my mother told me that they had to leave the university because members of the Karate club had caused some trouble.

It is interesting that even though Karate has a long history in Japan, schools (at the time) — from elementary to college — did not permit Karate clubs. Sometimes, students formed private clubs and practiced Karate at the corners of the school grounds, but these clubs were never recognized as a legitimate school activity and never received any funding. Also, members of these clubs often got into trouble, resulting in the suspension of their activities. Every time trouble occurred, it made big news in the local newspaper. Because of these problems, private *dojos* were popular.

There was a private Judo *dojo* near my home, headed by a well-known martial artist, but my friends attended a less-expensive class offered at my elementary school. Not wanting to be left out, I began to accompany them to class.

One day after I had started to accompany the older boys to Judo class, my father stopped me. "You've been coming home late lately. Where are you going every night?" I never doubted that he knew exactly what I was doing. Every day I told my mother about the older boys and Judo *dojo*. When I told my father I was going to Judo lessons, my older sisters interrupted. "Oh, no! Absolutely not! Forget Judo! If you practice Judo, your legs will be bowed. Try soccer or tennis. They are more popular in the States and Europe."

My sisters' view was one of two different views about physical education that were popular when I was young. One side believed that Japan should adopt Western sports and training methods for their childrens' physical education. The other side insisted that Japan's *Yamato damashii*, or *samurai* spirit, was the ideal method for teaching children. Japan has managed to combine these two points of view, and today both kinds of sports are enjoyed.

I didn't care either way. All I wanted to do was hang out with my older friends. They attended Judo classes, so I attended Judo classes. It would have been the same no matter what kind of classes they attended. One day my father asked me, "How are things at the Judo *dojo*?" I wasn't sure what he was driving at, but I was afraid he was going to tell me to stop. I told him I was going to Judo class every day. He didn't tell me to stop, but neither did he give me his permission.

My family waited a long time for me to ask my father for permission to practice Judo. Finally, they had to set the stage for me.

One day, my mother said, "If you really like practicing Judo, why don't you ask your father for permission?" My parents must have been talking about my Judo classes when I was away from home or asleep, though I never heard them. They never suggested that I begin training, even though they knew that I followed our group leader to Judo class every day. Looking back, I can understand what they were doing. They knew that if I asked them for permission to start Judo classes, I would be more determined to continue the training than if they suggested the idea to me.

They knew I needed my father's signature to become an official member of the Judo *dojo*. Eventually I had to ask my father to put his family seal — the Japanese equivalent of his signature — on a permission form. The form included an oath that said I would be a proud member of the Judo *dojo* and honor the principles of Judo, and would resign without hesitation if I ever caused any trouble or dishonor to the *dojo*. My father signed the form and I became an official Judo student. I had no uniform and had to practice in my street clothes, but I didn't mind.

This episode offers an interesting lesson about Japanese family life. In Japan, it's traditional for the mother to act as a mediator for a child who is seeking the father's permission to do something. Consequently, children naturally develop a warm, close relationship with their mothers, and a more distant, respectful relationship with their fathers.

After I joined the *dojo*, I was no longer subordinate to the leader of my group. Many students were older than he was, so he was not the leader at the *dojo*. It was a completely new world to me. Although I was a relatively young student, I was treated the same as the older kids. It was very tough. Participating in practice turned out to be a lot different — and a lot more difficult — than watching it.

We practiced in the gymnasium of our elementary school. Its wooden floor was glossy from years of washing and polishing. At the beginning of each class we swept and and washed the floor. Our cleaning tools were very different than the ones available today. The brooms were only a foot wide and had a three-foot long handle. Because we didn't have mops, we used rags. We would fill buckets with cold water, soak the wash rags in the water, wring them out and wash the floor by hand. There wasn't any hot water, which meant that washing the floor in the middle of winter was a painful task. We learned from older students to treat the rags gently when they were frozen to avoid breaking them. Sometimes — when we were lucky — the water pipes would freeze. Without running water, we couldn't wash the floor.

Our next task was to put *tatami* mats on the floor. *Tatami* mats are made of rice straw and are about six feet by three feet and two inches thick. A plant called "*Ai*" was used to create the heavily stitched coverings on the judo mats. The mats weren't light by any means, especially for younger students. Moisture and crushed corners were fatal injuries for *tatami* mats. To avoid such accidents, the younger students carried the mats in pairs, while the older, stronger students were allowed to carry mats by themselves. Younger students dreamed of the day when they could carry a mat by themselves.

Getting ready for class was quite a workout, and by the time the mats were in place, we were warmed up and stretched out. You might assume that our beginner's judo class began with lessons about falling and rolling. You would be wrong. It was only by falling and rolling many times that we learned to fall and roll. Our classes didn't include *ukemi* (falling and rolling) training, but because the games we had played as children included falling and rolling, it wasn't exactly new to us.

Six months after I became an official member of the Judo *dojo*, my parents bought me a new uniform. Looking back on it, I suspect that they waited six months because they wanted to make sure that I had a genuine interest in Judo. I'll never forget how happy I was. I took extremely good care of my prized possession. We didn't have a washing machine, so I had to scrub my uniform on a washing board using a bar of soap. It was made of extremely heavy material, which made wringing the water out after washing it another heavy-duty task. Being a small boy, I had to have my mother or sister help me with the task. I felt proud when I hung it on the second-floor balcony to dry and hoped that the neighbors would notice it.

When there were no Judo classes, I practiced Kendo (traditional sword techniques). An old man who taught sword fighting lived in my neighborhood. The protective equipment used in Kendo is very expensive, not something my family could afford at the time. Fortunately, my father found a set for me at a pawn shop. The chest armor was made of bamboo. Just a few pieces were missing. Training with this old man was very strict, and I recall being on the receiving end of many *shinai* (bamboo sword) strikes. One day, the old instructor suffered a stroke and my Kendo practice came to an abrupt end. More than anything else, I remember feeling relieved that I no longer had to attend his strenuous classes.

Seasonal training camps are a tradition in Japanese martial art practice. In the middle of winter and the middle of summer, *dojos* hold week-long camps. Of course, the week includes a normal school day for students and a normal work day for employees, so morning practice starts around six a.m. Schools, communities, and martial art associations all held training camps, and they coordinated the timing so anyone who wanted could attend all camps. At that time, there was no extra charge for attending these training camps, so I went to all of them. The most distant camp was hosted by the city of Akita. It took me an hour and a half to get there, so I had to leave home before five a.m. Winters were severe where I lived, and it was not unusual to have two- to three-foot snowfalls. You can imagine the sight of a young school boy walking to Judo practice at five a.m. in the morning through deep snow. Only newspaper delivery men were up at that hour.

On the cold winter days when I had to leave home before sunrise, getting up was the hardest task. My home didn't have central heating (it still doesn't), and the fire that heated the house during the day was extinguished at night for safety reasons. Outside of our *futons* (traditional Japanese bedding laid out on the floors for sleeping), the house was as cold as the weather outside.

After dragging myself out of my *futon* and getting dressed, I announced my departure by saying, *"Ittekimas."* (I am going now.) My father would say, *"Ki o tsukete"* (Take care of yourself) from his *futon*. My mother got up and checked my clothing. "Keep your warm scarf up! Put your gloves on right!" After making sure that I would survive the walk to the *dojo*, she would bid me farewell with a cheerful, *"Hai, ikinasai* (now, go)."

I would leave home and begin my trek. Soon, two or three friends joined me and we marched together to the *dojo*, leaning into the wind and blowing snow. Tall rubber boots stuffed with newspaper kept our feet warm and the snow out. When it was exceptionally cold, we used rice straw for insulation.

This scene may seem a little cold for some parents, but it's typical of Japanese child rearing. Many parents believe in the concept of "pushing loved ones away to give them opportunities to grow." As a child, I understood my parents' love, even though they never asked me about my practice or what I had learned. They showed their love in other ways. Every time I returned home, I was greeted with warm smiles and homemade snacks.

Five years ago, I asked my mother why she and my father never asked me about my practice. "We wanted you to have a clear separation between your Judo practice and the rest of your life," she said. "We didn't want you to get too involved in one thing. We wanted you to have a balanced education and to experience as many things as possible. Sometimes we encouraged you to do something you didn't like to do."

Although going to practice on cold winter mornings was quite an accomplishment in my eyes, my parents never offered any words of sympathy or praise. This may sound a little strange. Today, it's common for people to say, "Reward a child for good behavior." But when I was young, the discipline involved in Judo practice was not treated as something worthy of praise. My parents never said, "It must be hard for you to walk to the *dojo* in this cold weather," or "You are doing wonderfully." This concept that I learned early in life, that "practice wins no award" has become a fundamental principal at Nippon Kan.

This attitude allowed me to pursue anything, including my Judo training, without having to worry about whether or not I would get rewards from my parents. It was a pure form of training. I enjoyed it, and I quickly became skilled enough to participate in tournaments. I competed against students from other schools, but my parents never watched any of my tournaments. When I won, I would proudly bring my certificate home to show to my parents. My father would tell me to put it up on the *Shinto* altar in our best room. "You won because the gods were on your side today," he would say as a reminder that I shouldn't become too impressed with myself.

One time, our team entered a tournament to decide who would represent Akita City in an upcoming regional tourney. It was a very important day for our team and for me. My parents hadn't said anything about coming to the tournament, but during warm-ups, I caught a glimpse of my father talking to our coach. He quickly disappeared — before my bout. Later, the coach told me that my father had come to watch the tournament, but he was so worried about my bout that he had to leave. The coach added, "For your father, do your best!"

A few days later, my father told me a slightly different story. "If I had stayed and watched, you might have been even more nervous than you already were, or you might have tried too hard to please me. I wanted you to do your best for yourself; not for me. That's why I left. I did want to watch, though." I was glad to know that he wanted to watch me perform but had decided not to stay because he was thinking of what was best for me. Many years later, I find that I am still learning about my parents' love for me and I appreciate them — and my good fortune — even more.

We won the tournament, and I received a certificate. When I told him what had happened, my father said, "I see." To my father, a man born in the *Meiji* era (1868–1912), a martial art tournament was not about winning and losing, nor was it about trophies and certificates. That's a much different attitude than you find in many parents and martial art *dojos* today.

Today, there is a great deal of emphasis on rewards. The winners at martial art tournaments receive many rewards — a promotion in rank, a different color belt, not to mention ribbons, medals, and trophies. After a tournament victory, parents shower their children with praise and presents. "You did well." "You were wonderful!" "Next month there's another, bigger tournament." And so on. Parents often give their children praise and prizes when the children do things that the parents wish they had done themselves. When children are totally motivated by reward, they are no longer free to pursue things that genuinely interest them.

My parents worried that I would turn into a child who was motivated only by praise and prizes. That is why they pretended that they were not concerned about my martial art practice. I think it takes great courage to place one's children under such emotional discipline, but being members of a traditional Japanese household it was considered part of normal child rearing. My parents were traditional and conservative, my father being a shrine keeper and an army officer; the most traditional of occupations. I grew up in an environment in which the traditional Japanese spirit was strictly maintained.

Today in Japan life has, of course, changed. Modern problems such as instructor's time constraints, liability, and teachers unions have made martial arts in schools for younger children far less available. Martial art *dojos* today are mostly private or run by community programs. Kids and their young parents are more influenced by fads than educational tradition. Movies and television make Judo *dojos* popular for a time, and there is a cartoon series on T.V. featuring Kendo. There is even a Japanese version of "Karate Kid" called "Best Kid." All of these indicating a shift in Japan from the values of men like my father toward a more material and media- oriented world of today. On that note, I would like to turn the scene from my childhood to the children's Aikido courses at Nippon Kan.

DON'T USE YOUR CHILD
TO MAKE A DEAL

Earlier, I wrote about a few of the common telephone calls Nippon Kan receives from parents. Of course, parents frequently show up at the *dojo* without warning to see about the classes we offer. For example, one day, a child who had never been to the *dojo* ran onto the mat before we had a chance to ask who he was or where his parents were. His father appeared a few moments later. Another time, a father entered the *dojo* with his young son attached to his leg, peeking out timidly. We have had entire families drop by unannounced — mom, dad, and all the kids on a family outing. We have also been visited by more than one kid dressed up as a turtle.

At Nippon Kan, the ten a.m. Saturday class is the largest children's class. Parents often show up with their children at the beginning of this class to begin their Aikido training. Their first exchange takes place at the office window. Variations of the following conversation occur quite often:

"Hello, I want to enroll my son in Aikido class."

"Fine. Please fill out a registration form and a liability form. Our monthly dues are $20."

"Hmm? I'm not sure if my boy is going to continue that long. Could he try one class without charge?"

"I'm sorry, but we don't offer free classes at this *dojo*."

"But other *dojos* are offering one free trial lesson. Why not here?"

I can understand his concern. If you open up the yellow pages to the Martial Arts section, you will find that many *dojos* offer free trial lessons. While this may be a good marketing tactic, I do not do this at Nippon Kan. My reason is very simple: If a parent or any potential student is seriously interested in finding a suitable *dojo*, they would not ask for one free trial lesson. In my experience, for we have tried it in the past, parents or students who asked for free lessons never come back. They found the class entertaining but they were not seriously interested in learning Aikido.

It's not that I don't value new customers. The success of a martial arts *dojo* depends on the students who attend classes. The more new students, the healthier a *dojo* will be, especially small *dojos*. As a result, many martial art *dojos* have developed sales pitches based on a "free lesson."

When parents first approach a *dojo*, they have many questions. "Will my child be all right in class? Is the instructor competent and kind? Will my child get along with the other children?" Some schools require new students to purchase uniforms and sign lengthy contracts; parents become quite nervous if asked to sign anything before getting answers to these questions. The free trial class offered at some *dojos* is a sales technique to allay parent's concerns and to get them to make lengthy commitments. Rather than being a class, this trial lesson is usually a demonstration.

First, the students cheerfully demonstrate the skills they have been practicing. Then the instructor and his students impress the parents with unbelievable techniques. Parents are led to believe that their child will quickly be able to perform as well as the children in the demonstration. One commonly used trick in such Aikido demonstrations is the "unmoveable body." In this demonstration, a child student is told by the instructor to stand relaxed. He says: "If you can relax completely, no one can move you. Watch this." He then pushes the student with exaggerated movements, actually applying very little direct pressure. Of course the student doesn't move.

Prospective young students are entertained with these dramatic demonstrations; parents are delighted that their children are sitting quietly. When the instructor explains children will develop greater concentration through Aikido training, that's about all it takes to convince many parents to sign a contract. This kind of free lesson is a sure-fire way to attract new students, but it's not something you will find at Nippon Kan. At Nippon Kan, parents are free to watch a practice with their children; to ask questions of me and my staff; to read our literature; to talk with other parents. If that's not enough information to make a decision, a free lesson isn't going to make a difference.

Sometimes financial matters prevent a child from studying Aikido. I'll tell you a story about how a small financial matter led to a parting of ways.

Not long ago, a man began attending adult classes at the same time he enrolled his children in our children's class. After a few month's he showed up one morning wanting to talk to somebody about his dues. "My children came three times last month, not four times," he said. "You should take $5 off my bill. I shouldn't have to pay a full month's dues."

We told him that continuing students paid a monthly fee, regardless of the number of classes they attend. He seemed to understand, but instead of dropping the matter, he began to plead his case to other parents. Some of these parents had been sending their children to class for years. They all understood and accepted our fee structure. The unhappy parent wasn't having much success collecting allies. Finally, I intervened. "What is it you really want?" I asked.

"I'm sending three children to private schools, and it costs a lot. My business costs have been rising; and so have my insurance bills. We are financially stricken," he answered.

What could I say to this? I thought for a moment. He had enough money to send his children to private schools, but he couldn't afford $35 a month for his two children's' Aikido classes. "What you have to do is to cut expenses, maybe by reducing your activities," I said. "In your financial condition, you won't be happy about sending your children to this *dojo*. Maybe you can find a *dojo* that is sympathetic to your situation." That was the end of his affiliation with Nippon Kan.

Parents who try to negotiate fees are not the worst that we have seen: There have actually been a couple of cases when parents have tried to sneak their children into class without notifying the front office. Most parents understand that a martial arts *dojo* has financial obligations to meet. Other parents are more interested in cutting a deal than in finding the best *dojo* for their children. This is why I don't offer free trial lessons, and I don't make special deals with parents. I simply try to offer high-quality classes at the lowest possible price. I sincerely hope that concerned parents will be able to discern a *dojo*'s principle philosophies — administrative as well as educational — when shopping for a place to educate their children.

DO YOUR HOMEWORK BEFORE YOU CHOOSE A SCHOOL

The current trend in Aikido *dojos* is for instructors to hold traditional full-time jobs while they teach Aikido classes and work out on the side. They're happy if they can make enough money through the school to pay for the rented space and the mats. They teach because they enjoy teaching; not because they need to teach to make money. Other instructors have truly made a lifetime commitment to teaching Aikido and own their own *dojos*. For those instructors who have made a lifetime commitment to teaching a martial art, making money and operating a successful *dojo* are secondary. First, they are in the business of human relations.

If I were looking for a good martial art *dojo* for my child, I would choose a *dojo* whose instructors fit the descriptions in the previous paragraph. Unfortunately, the advertisements you see for martial arts *dojos* emphasize points that don't have anything to do with quality. Often, a *dojo* will hype its affiliation with a national or international organization, "Member of the XYZ International Federation." Many ads offer "$19.95 Introductory Specials!" You may even get a genuine martial art uniform.

Think about it. How much does it cost to run this kind of ad? How many new students does it take each month to pay for these ads? How stable is this *dojo* as a business? The only way it can survive is by recruiting lots of students. A *dojo* that is totally dependent on attracting new students is usually a *dojo* that doesn't have many continuing students.

Parents looking for a martial arts *dojo* are often in such a hurry to part with their money that they often don't bother to find out what they're buying. I remember a man who brought his two sons to my *dojo*. He didn't ask a single question about the *dojo* or about Aikido, instead his question was, "How much for two children?"

"Our fee is $20 a month for one child, $15 for additional children; additional family members ..."

He wasn't interested in discounts. "Okay, okay. Do they need uniforms and patches like the other children are wearing? How much? I would like to pay for six months of dues in advance."

Finally, I had to say, "Wait, wait, please. If you pay six months' dues for your children and a month from now they tell you that they don't like it, what will you do? Why don't you watch a class and see what Aikido is?"

"Well, thank you, but it's too much trouble to pay every month. I'll go ahead and pay now."

"Why don't you pay for a month, then, if your children enjoy Aikido, you can buy uniforms for them."

Finally, he agreed and paid only one month's dues. The next week, his children showed up for class in brand new uniforms. I have no doubt that he paid a lot more for the uniforms than he would have had he waited a month and bought them from us, but he couldn't wait that long and money was no object.

Some *dojos* are in the business of selling colored belts as a way to pay the bills. Traditionally, colored belts are used in martial art *dojos* to indicate how long the wearer of a certain color has been practicing. The color of the belt is also an indication of the wearer's skill level. Unfortunately, some parents think that colored belts are a matter of choice and money. I have had many parents of new students ask, "How much for a purple belt?" How much for a green belt?"

I can't blame them for asking. If you go to some martial arts *dojos*, you'll find a chart that explains how the colors of the belts relate to class fees. "Green belt, $50.00, two months." Blue belt, $200, four months." And so on. These schools conduct "testing" at the end of a a set of classes and award the students the belt they paid for. Such *dojos* are in the business of selling colored belts.

I have even seen ads that show a seven- or eight-year-old child wearing a martial art uniform with a black belt! Such ads are impossible for me to understand. How can a seven-year old have trained long enough and be mature enough to achieve what is traditionally the highest rank awarded in martial arts? You would never see this kind of ad in Japan.

But it's not the parents who are at fault here. They have no way of knowing that schools that emphasize advancing through a series of belts — for a set fee — may not offer high-quality instruction.

At Nippon Kan, colored belts are used to distinguish the skills of a broad range of students. The color of a student's belt indicates the level of training that student has attained. The colored belts have a very simple purpose: To let instructors and the students know the relative skill levels of the students. This doesn't mean that one color is "better" than another. Generally, the color of a student's belt is an indication of how long the student has been taking classes. Because Aikido classes at Nippon Kan don't include examinations, promotion to a different color belt does not depend on testing; it depends on ability.

When selecting a martial art *dojo* for your child — or for yourself for that matter — carefully observe the instructors and the rest of the staff. If you are at a good *dojo*, the instructors and the staff will observe you as carefully as you observe them. Keep in mind that although many martial art *dojos* use the word "school" in their name, it doesn't mean that they have met any official requirements. Many of these *"dojos"* rent a small space with a big front window that faces a busy street. It's easy for passers-by to catch glimpses of classes. Martial art trophies are prominently displayed in the window, colored belts, flags and flashy posters hang from the walls.

The instructors are young men in their mid-twenties who hold double-digit black belts in a number of styles. *Dojos* like this come and go faster than you can say, "How much for black belt?" Many disappear after collecting many months worth of fees from students. I did a mailing a few years back to all of the martial art *dojos* in Colorado — there were more than seventy *dojos* listed. Six months later, about a third of them no longer existed. Yet, the telephone books still listed about the same number as there had been six months earlier. The *dojos* that had gone under had been replaced by new schools.

I'm afraid that "instant" martial art *dojos* have given all martial art *dojos* a terrible reputation. I've heard so many horror stories about martial art *dojos*, I can understand why the general public has a negative perception. For someone like me who has devoted his life to teaching a martial art it's very sad to hear these stories. However, I believe that there are still many instructors who operate financially stable, high-quality, traditional *dojos*.

If you are looking for a first-class martial art *dojo*, you should ask the following questions:

- How old are the students?
- What is the range of ages of the students in a class?
- Are the class fees reasonable?
- How old and how experienced are the instructors?
- How do students behave in class and outside of class?
- Is there sufficient equipment and is it well maintained?
- How long has the *dojo* been in business?

You have the right to choose a martial art *dojo* that suits your requirements and meets your standards. If you can find a *dojo* whose goals for its students match your goals for your children, you have found a good *dojo*.

WHEN IT'S TIME TO SAY GOODBYE

When students join the children's class at Nippon Kan, they are asked to leave their shoes at the entrance of the *dojo*. This is an ancient tradition in Japan, where the inside of a house is clearly distinguished from the outside. Shoes are worn outside; they are removed when you enter a house. More specifically, it is traditional to remove your shoes in the entranceway, just inside the front door of a Japanese house. In some homes, slippers are provided at the entranceway to replace shoes. No doubt, this habit developed naturally over time as a way to maintain sanitary conditions in Japan's humid climate. But removing one's shoes at the door of a house has a deeper significance.

As children, we were taught that evil things stuck to the soles of our shoes. To keep these evil things from getting into anybody's house, we were instructed to carefully remove our shoes before entering. And that wasn't all. After you remove your shoes, you must place them so that the toes point toward the outside. Evil things must not be directed toward the inside of a house.

At school, Japanese children learn early that removing one's shoes upon entering a house and placing them properly after taking them off is a very serious matter. Our parents made it clear that children from a proper home are always neat, and they always take off their shoes and place them neatly — toes facing out— when they enter someone's house. It is a popular Zen saying that if you cannot even line up your shoes, it will be difficult to find order in the world around you.

Why all of this information about the Japanese tradition of removing your shoes when you enter someone's house? I'll get back to that in a moment.

I can't say for sure, but I imagine that the night before a child's first Aikido class is filled with excitement. When a child is looking forward to something new, it can't happen soon enough. "What time are we leaving in the morning?" "Did you set your alarm, just in case?" "What time does class start?"

After several weeks of practice, things often change drastically. Children are not always as animated as they were for their first class. Occasionally, they move slowly. They have their ups and downs, this is only natural for children. I remember one boy who was so excited on his first day of practice that he dashed from his father's arms onto the mat. One morning many weeks later, he clung to his father and was reluctant to practice. He was behaving like a completely different child.

It's not always easy for a child to get up and get ready on a Saturday morning for a 10:00 Aikido class. Plus, there are cartoons on television, and their friends are doing other things. Children are children, and they don't always want to spend their Saturday mornings in a martial arts class. One thing that we try to make parents understand from the beginning is that they shouldn't drag a reluctant child to Aikido class.

Let me explain. Many times, I have seen parents carry their sleepy children to the *dojo*. Although these parents have done quite a bit of work to get their children to class, I don't think they're helping their children develop good habits. If they have to provide the motivation for their children to attend class, their children will try to find out how far they can push them. Pretty soon, what began as well-intentioned nudging (carrying a drowsy child) becomes a discussion. Finally it turns into "Let's Make a Deal." In the worst case, parents end up making deals with their children to get them to attend class.

Which brings me back to the tradition of removing your shoes upon entering a Japanese house.

Sometimes parents nudge their children into class by offering to help them take off their jacket and shoes. The agreement, whether spoken or not, is this: I'll help you take off your jacket and shoes, if you will be a good child and go to class.

This is the same as saying, "If you go to school, we'll buy you a new bicycle." If reward is a child's motivation, the child will come to expect more and bigger rewards. Eventually, no reward is big enough, and the child has no motivation.

I try to avoid this situation by making it clear from the beginning that new students are expected to do a few things on their own to prepare for class. When a new student arrives, I usually greet the student with, "Good morning!" using my best made-in-Japan English.

Often, new students are shy and and don't respond right away.

"Good morning!" I say again.

Eventually, even a shy student will return my greeting. Once the ice is broken, I begin to introduce the student to some of the rules of the *dojo*.

"Before you get on to the mat, you'll have to take off your shoes and socks and put them in the shoe rack. And make sure you fold your jacket neatly and put it away before going into the *dojo*." I make it clear that the student, not the parents, is expected to take care of these tasks.

As they watch their children awkwardly trying to do what they have been told, some parents have the urge to help. I try to make it clear that the children are expected to do these things by themselves, but sometimes parents don't get my message and help their children get ready. When this happens, I wait until the children are practicing and tell the parents, "Please, let your child get ready by herself. It doesn't matter how long it takes." I don't usually go into detail, and parents don't always understand my reasoning at first. Sometimes it takes a while for them to realize that requiring children to prepare themselves for classes is part of Aikido training and helps develop self-reliance. On the other hand, after parents begin to understand the approach we use, they don't require an explanation for everything we do.

If children can motivate themselves to attend class and learn to get themselves ready, parents won't end up having to make deals to get them to participate. When it's finally time for the children to begin class, we encourage them to hug their parents and say goodbye. Then it's time for Aikido practice.

NO OBSERVATION SEATS
FOR PARENTS

At Nippon Kan, the area where students work out is clearly separated from the lobby. This isn't the case with many martial art *dojos*, where an observation area is connected to the work-out area. In Japan, the place where martial arts are practiced is traditionally considered a place for education. It is not therefore appropriate to allow observers, especially observers who are chatting amongst themselves, drinking their morning coffee, or reading the newspaper. In Japan, this no-observers tradition includes parents except for special occasions. I have found that this tradition has not survived in many American martial art *dojos*, where parents often watch their children practice.

We are careful to explain to all new students and their parents that our *dojo* is not a gymnasium; it's a school. It is a place for teaching and learning. It is not a gym where spectators watch the instructors as they teach and students as they learn. Parents of beginning students are often surprised — and not particularly happy — with this policy. They assume they would be allowed to watch their children practice martial arts as they would baseball or soccer practice.

I don't often explain the details of this policy, saying only that the *dojo* area is a place for education and that even in America, it's not customary for parents to watch their children during school. However, there are other reasons that our *dojo* doesn't include an observation area for parents.

After saying goodbye to one another, the children go into the *dojo*, and the parents remain in the lobby, or run errands, etc. Children use the time before class to run and play on the mat with their classmates. Within a few minutes of free play, they often change drastically, finding their places in their own world. The workout area is covered by a big, soft mat where children are free to run and jump and roll and play as much as they like (under the careful, but passive, supervision of the instructors). Children, who only moments before were shy under the watchful eye of their parents, turn into little balls of energy when left to interact as children do in a children's world.

In the early years of Nippon Kan, I allowed parents to watch children's classes. But it didn't take me long to notice that, when under their parent's eye, children often had difficulty concentrating on what they were doing and seemed somewhat nervous and distracted. While this may not be true for all children, I found that they would often look toward their parents to make sure they were watching, to make sure their actions were approved of.

During exercises the children race while mimicking the movements of animals; doing the duck walk, the rabbit hop etc. (see part III) When parents were present, we have seen the children that won the races wave happily to their parents while the children who were a little slower looked over apologetically, sometimes attempting to find something to blame for their "failure." Aikido techniques are mostly practiced with partners. Students behave much differently as they practice with each other if their parents are watching. Some students are much rougher, throwing their partners down as if they were enemies, then looking for an approving smile from their parents. A nod from a parent at that point is the kind of reinforcement that sends exactly the wrong message to a child training in a martial art.

The attention and praise that children receive from their parents strongly affects their behavior. I believe that there comes a time in a child's development when it is best not to have parents physically present — a time when a child learns to behave independent of their parents' will and supervision.

I remember one child in particular, a boy about six years old. He arrived at the *dojo* in the arms of his father, who told me his son was very shy. The boy wore a brand-new uniform and clutched a large transformer toy. When it was time for class to begin, the boy wouldn't leave his father. Finally, after they talked for a while, the boy agreed to go to class if he could take his toy. While the other children practiced, the new student stayed in a corner playing with his toy. Occasionally, he would run to the lobby — toy in hand — to show his father what new shape he had created. His father gave him praise and encouragement.

After a while, I asked the child to leave the toy in the lobby and asked his father to come into the work-out area to watch his son practice. But the boy was more concerned with keeping his father's attention than practicing, and he never took his eyes off his father.

The next week, we asked the father to watch only the beginning of class and wait in the lobby for the rest of the hour. The boy immediately noticed when his father was no longer watching and went to the lobby to look for him. The child then wouldn't return to class until he was allowed to take his toy. When he returned to the work-out area, he again sat in the corner and played. Soon he was running back to the lobby to show his father the new shape he had created and to receive a dose of praise and encouragement — things that he didn't receive for practicing Aikido.

I don't mean to say that praise and encouragement are bad for a child. Certainly the opposite is true: All children need their parents' support. But if taken too far, support can lead to dependence. We were unable to separate the child from his toy. We also couldn't separate him from his father long enough to participate in class. I suppose this situation could be viewed as a strong parent-child relationship, but I didn't see it that way.

Eventually, I decided to introduce the "no observation" policy. Things quickly changed. I found that children behaved quite differently than they did when their parents were watching. They were less nervous and more eager to participate. Concentration and the quality of the classes, improved.

Obviously, this policy doesn't mean that all classes are always closed to everybody. We allow visiting relatives or out-of town guests to watch class. Promotion ceremonies and other special events are open to parents. But for general classes, parents are expected to wait in the lobby or pick their children up after class.

While we don't permit parents to watch their children during class, we do place a great deal of importance on the role they play in their childrens' Aikido development. After all, it is the parents who choose to enroll their children in class, and it's the parents who bring their children to class, pick them up, and provide encouragement when their children need it. When a child is nervous, for example, we encourage parents to provide reassurance that they will be right there waiting for them when class is over.

We know that our no observation policy asks a great deal of parents, but we believe that this approach enables parents to focus on a supportive roll in their children's martial arts training. We can teach Aikido, but only if the children are brought to the *dojo* and encouraged.

I have written much about what I think is the proper involvement of parents in children's classes which, as I mentioned, is heavily influenced by traditional Japanese methods. In the next chapter, I will tell you a little more about the education that I received as a child in Japan and how it has influenced my view of how children should be taught martial arts.

EDUCATION WITHOUT EMOTION

The teaching style of all martial arts instructors is a reflection of their background. I, for example, am a born-in Japan instructor who uses made-in Japan English. While my English is not equal to that of my American-born counterparts, I have one credential they don't have — a Japanese upbringing and first-hand knowledge of Japanese traditions. My background is certainly reflected in my teaching style.

For some parents who enroll their children in a Japanese martial arts class, it is important to find an instructor with a traditional Japanese background. For these parents, whether or not the instructor is "made in Japan" is an important factor. If I taught Aikido using a completely American approach, my students wouldn't get the benefit of my heritage.

I remember visiting the zoo a few years ago. As I read the signs that identified the animals, I thought that it would be interesting if people wore similar identification tags. Mine would say: "Gaku Homma: Race — Mongolian; Nationality — Japanese; Sex — male; Occupation — martial artist." The thought made me laugh, but it's an accurate description. Many occasions have reminded me that I am, indeed, a "Mongolian Japanese male martial artist."

My parents were born in the *Meiji* period (1868–1912). This was a very traditional period before any major influences from the West. My father was a shrine keeper and an army officer. My mother was a well-educated, true *Meiji* woman. I was born after World War II — a Japanese baby-boomer. My family had little money, but like most families of that time, they maintained the *samurai* tradition when it came to raising their children.

Japan — and all the world — has experienced rapid change during my lifetime. I have often wondered about the impact that these changes will have on Japanese traditions. I have also spent a lot of time thinking about the best approach for teaching a martial art in the United States. I see two choices: A "modern" approach, a more broad-appeal, commercialized style of instruction; and a "classical" approach, to teach Aikido as I learned it, complete with all its Japanese traditions.

(These days, you find "classical" things in a museum, and perhaps that's where I belong.)

I decided long ago that it wouldn't be fair to the parents who were searching for traditional Japanese martial art instruction if I used only a commercialized approach when teaching Aikido. I concluded that it was best to stick with my classical approach, to become a living museum exhibition and provide a place where students could come and learn about the traditions I grew up with. To uphold those traditions, we don't hold tournaments, we don't award trophies, we don't put on flashy demonstrations, and the children who attend our classes don't cover their uniforms with patches. For some parents, colored belts, trophies, patches, and other material rewards are important; they usually aren't attracted to Aikido. On the other hand, the parents who seek something more, who feel that traditional Japanese instruction can offer a unique perspective, are often attracted to Aikido.

Let me explain a bit about the exhibit titled "Gaku Homma" and how he came to be the exhibit he is. I think it is important to look at some of the differences between the way I was raised and the way I have seen children being raised today here in the United States. Before I begin, I should warn you that my background, and therefore my outlook, is probably much different that yours. I ask that you not be judgmental. I also don't mean to imply that the way I was brought up in Japan is better than an American way; only that it's different.

As I mentioned earlier, my parents were raised in a traditional manner prior to the post-war democratic reforms, and they raised their children the same way. Although my father was very strict, he scolded me only once severely that I can remember. However, I was scolded by my mother. The way in which we were both scolded and praised was quite different than in America. At that time in a traditional Japanese family, educating and caring for the children was the sole responsibility of the mother. The father's duty was to earn a living. At that time the householder had absolute authority over and legal possession of all members of the family. After the war, the male household heads lost this ownership, but the traditional attitude still lingers.

My mother and father were older than my classmates' parents. I still remember once that when all of the mothers came to visit our school, they all had nice Western clothes; my mother was the only one in a traditional Japanese *kimono*. She was also the only mother who was older than my homeroom teacher.

Once in a great while, I see a few of the classmates with whom I spent my elementary school days. When we talk about "the good old days" it becomes very apparent that there is a great deal of difference even between the way in which we were raised in Japan and the way children are being raised today in Japan. Something we all agree on was that there was not a lot of praise given to children in those days.

To be honest, I don't remember ever receiving praise from my parents. That does not mean I never did anything worthy of praise. I did well in martial art tournaments, and I was well behaved at school and at home. On many occasions, I brought home certificates for good performance. My parent's reaction to these awards was quite different from the way most parents today would react. For example, when I reported to them that I had earned praise from my teacher, my father would say, "I see," and my mother would make a similar remark. That was all. One day I brought home a certificate that I had won at school for my summer project. My mother said, "I'm happy for you. Put it on the *Kamidana* (house shrine)." She didn't seem too excited about it, and I don't remember receiving any hugs or affection. The meaning behind my mother's words was, "Put your reward on the *Kamidana* because it was not your ability alone that won the certificate; the gods helped you." It was her way of keeping me from becoming too impressed with myself.

I participated in athletic competitions each spring and fall during elementary school. There were not many other recreational activities in those days, and these sporting events were special times that parents and children could enjoy together.

I remember waking up before six a.m. on the day of the competition and listening for the fireworks that heralded the big event. The sports day was a volunteer day for the parents — fathers went to the school to help set up for the event and mothers cooked lunches. There were many children whose fathers couldn't get out of work on Sundays; other families couldn't afford to provide food, but nonetheless, it was a major event for the community.

I was an athletic kid and did very well in the competition. Every time I would win a certificate, I would take it to my parents who were watching. When I handed them the certificate, they would say, "The day is not over yet, and there is more for you to do. It is too early for you to feel at ease." Their response was a reflection of the traditional Japanese approach to raising children — parents simply did not express joy and pride in public, no matter what their children accomplished. Tradition called for all children to be treated equally. Therefore, parents could not display any sort of favoritism — even toward their own children. Instead, they lectured their children about not becoming overconfident and egotistical and they emphasized that we should concentrate on what we had left to do; not on what we had already done.

Children learned to take encouragement from their parent's advice. If our parents had said, "Congratulations, you did well," it would have sent the message that we could relax; that the challenge was over. On the other hand, when they said things like, "It's not over, yet, so you can't let up," it encouraged us to try even harder.

There came a time when I became the leader of the neighborhood children's group. When I reported this great honor to my parents, their response was,"Do you really think you can handle the responsibility?" Their words were hardly encouraging, but they challenged and motivated me. Their response may sound a little cold — it seemed cold to me at the time — but what they were actually telling me was to take my new responsibility seriously and do my very best.

I didn't begin to understand the reasons behind my parents' actions until I was in my thirties. A few years ago when I was visiting Japan, my aunt told me something confidentially: "Every time you received a reward, your mother would visit us and tell us the whole story. She worried about you as the youngest child of a family without much money. Your parents couldn't provide much in the way of material goods for you, but they hoped that you'd grow up to be a good man and maintain the tradition and stature of the Homma family. They didn't understand the new, modern ways of education, but they tried to follow the recommendations of your teachers. They decided that the best thing they could do for you was to show the way they walked with confidence. They were happy when you did well in competition and when you became the neighborhood children's leader. But they were also very worried that you might make a serious mistake. They worried that when you took Judo lessons you might not do your school homework. They worried that you might get hurt." My aunt talked at length about my parents' concern for me. Although on the outside their treatment of me seemed rather cold, the fact is that they were concerned about my growth and proud of my accomplishments. I had thought that my parents did not feel many emotions good or bad, but the fact was they were expressing joy and concern where I couldn't see it. Rather than express their true feelings to me, they expressed them to my aunts and uncles.

"That is the spirit of the *Meiji* era," said my aunt.

WHEN I WAS SCOLDED

It may seem to you that my upbringing was unusually strict, but most of the children of *Meiji*-era parents were raised in a similar fashion. These parents thought of their children as members of society first and members of the family second. Our parents had been raised in the *Meiji* tradition, and they passed this tradition on to their children. The *Meiji* spirit is the foundation of Japan's current economic prosperity. Again, I want to remind you that I am not trying to say that Japanese customs are better or worse than American customs; I am simply telling you what it was like to grow up in post-war Japan. I mentioned earlier that my style of teaching is a reflection of my upbringing. I hope that by telling you a little about my own education you will better understand where my attitudes come from, and how my upbringing differed from the kind I have found in the United States.

I don't recall getting scolded too often as a child. In general, my parents were strict and discipline was maintained. I do recall that my parents often cautioned me — about being careful and about how to act as a proper member of society — but I was never punished or scolded for getting into fights with other kids. The leader of our neighborhood group was responsible for making sure that nobody got hurt, so parents did not interfere in those matters.

I remember one incident in which I definitely crossed the line, breaking a rule of judgement and character that found me facing a lesson my whole family felt I needed to learn.

We used to play a card game called *"Menko,"* which was the most popular game among boys of my generation. The cards were round and made of thick cardboard; usually with pictures or drawings of children's heroes. Players took turns placing cards down; the objective was to flip or push out the other players' cards.

Some cards — the ones with the best pictures — were more valuable than others; some were collector's items. But even if someone had a particularly good card they had to play it. Simply owning it wasn't enough; you had to play it and risk losing it. The player who won the most and best cards had bragging rights — and possession. One day — I don't know if I was good or my opponent was simply unlucky — I ended up with many cards, and I took my winnings home with me.

Later that day, the boy whose cards I had won showed up at our door accompanied by his mother. They demanded that I return the cards. She especially wanted me to return the ones that had her son's favorite characters. My mother called me to the door and asked, "What happened today? What did you do to the boy?" I explained what had happened and emphasized that I had won the cards "fair and square" according to the rules of *Menko*. My mother wasn't convinced.

"You have so many cards," she said. "And you took new cards from a younger boy. That isn't fair. Why don't you return some of them?" I was not happy at all and tried very hard to make my mother understand the situation as I understood it.

Finally, I became so angry that I threw all the cards at the other boy's mother. My mother slapped me. My mother had been handling the situation very calmly, but when I threw the cards she changed dramatically.

Shocked, I ran back into my room and cried. Later, my mother came to my room and gave me a very harsh lecture. "It is outrageous to assault someone's parent, regardless of the reason." Spanking a child is not a Japanese tradition, but pinching was, and my mother pinched my inner thigh for what seemed a very long time.

When my older brother and sisters came home later and heard about what had happened, my brother came to my room offering sympathy. My sisters visited later and kindly told me that I should not have acted violently. At the time I didn't stop to think about why my brother and sisters visited me. It wasn't until well into my thirties that I realized that my brother and sisters were following my mother's instructions to teach me to look at things from different perspectives and to make the best possible decisions.

I remember worrying about what would happen when my father learned about the incident. I didn't want him to find out. My brother suggested that I apologize to my mother so that she wouldn't tell my father. My sisters came to my room again to ask if I was hungry: Their real motive was to get me out of my room and into the dining room, where I would have to face my mother. Persuaded by my siblings, I apologized to my mother. She then said to me, "If your father finds out about what you did, I would be in trouble also. So I won't tell him about what happened. But if you do that again, I will have to report to your father. Your brother and sisters have asked me to forgive you, so I do. Case closed."

If my father had found out that I had taken advantage of a younger boy, he wouldn't have been interested in my side of the story. I would have been in for a severe scolding and possibly more.

I also remember that as a child, I feared getting into trouble by accidentally hurting myself. Ever since I was old enough to understand my parents' words, I was told repeatedly that I must take good care of myself. My body was given to me by God, and it was absolutely sacrilegious to hurt myself.

One day while sharpening a pencil with my knife I accidentally cut my finger. In a situation like this, you might assume that my mother ran to me asking if I was all right. This wasn't the case. The first thing my mother said, or rather shouted, was, "What a terrible thing you just did!" Before expressing any sympathy, she scolded me for doing such a thing to my own body. Every day we were taught to cherish and take care of our bodies.

I remember being scolded only once by my father. As I mentioned earlier, my father was very strict when it came to managing the house and raising his children. However, he rarely had to intervene in domestic problems. The other family members were expected to handle whatever problems arose by themselves. It was a matter of his pride and authority.

When I was nineteen years old, a dinner discussion with my brother about my future escalated into a fight. I had been an Aikido student for many years, and my brother was relatively skinny and unathletic, so I was dominating the fight, which consisted of grappling and rolling around rather than kicking and punching. Although my sisters tried to stop us, it was my uncle from next door who eventually broke us up. By the time we were pulled apart, the room was a mess and my clothes were torn.

During the fight, my father never said a word or moved from his place. When it ended, I straightened myself and started walking out of the room. That was when my father's thunderous voice rang out. "You idiot! How is it that you brothers fought in front of your parents? It is a shameful action. I did not let you take martial art lessons so you could beat up on your own brother. If you want to fight, why don't you come after me!" he said, rising to his feet.

My mother rushed in to hold him back, my uncle tried to calm him down, and my sisters stood between us. I got scared, and left the house — quickly. Following the fighting incident, I didn't return home for more than a year.

That was the only time that I was scolded by my father. He felt very strongly that brothers shouldn't fight, but it was a different story when I got into a fight with the leader of a rival neighborhood group. One time the parent of a boy with whom I had gotten into a fist fight showed up at our house to complain. My brother and sisters and I were eating dinner at the time, so we could all hear the discussion. My father listened to the visitor, but he had no intention of getting involved in the case. It was mother's responsibility to deal with neighbors. After the visitor left, my mother said that she felt that I deserved a good lecture, and she started to press the issue. My father told her, "Take it easy now. We are eating our dinner. Scolding can wait until later." Turning to me, he asked, "By the way, did you win or not?"

After the dinner, my father started reading the paper. I was not certain at all where the line had been drawn, but I got the message that some actions warranted scolding and punishment while others didn't merit a heavy penalty. I can recall three actions that resulted in scoldings: 1) picking on children who were weaker than I; 2) treating my brother and sisters badly; and 3) not taking care of my body and health.

In 1986, in my mid thirties, I returned home and for the first time drank *sake* in front of my father. I had brought a bottle home with me, but I was only allowed a single glass. When I tried to pour myself a second, my father said to me quietly, "Don't die before me." My father had already seen three of his sons die — two before I was born and my older brother, who had died a few years earlier. Coming from him, it was a very powerful statement.

One evening not long after that, my father — who normally didn't drink — offered me a cup and poured himself one. After taking a small sip, he asked if things were going well for me. I was not expecting such friendly words from him, even though I knew he was concerned about how I was doing. Before that time, I had had to talk to my father from *seiza* (a formal sitting position with one's feet crossed under the buttocks, back straight) from a distance of about six feet. The evening when he offered me a cup of *sake* was the turning point of our relationship. Since then, my father has told me much about the history and the principles of the Homma family and about the family's future. The death of my older brother left the responsibility of carrying on our family's traditions to me.

A year later I again visited Japan and my parents' house. When I arrived home, my mother was in front of the house dressed in her new *kimono* waiting to greet the head of the family — me. A few days later when it was time for me to leave, she walked out the front gate with me and bowed deeply to me to say good-bye. She kept her head down until she could no longer see the taxi that was taking me to the airport. It is very special for a Japanese mother to bow to her son. By doing so, my mother was recognizing me as the head of the Homma family.

When I look at pictures of me at three or four years old, I see no difference between them and family pictures of friends of mine in America, I was held in my mother's arms or played in my father's lap. There came the time, however, when my education as a young Japanese male began, and such intimacy was left behind forever.

As you can see from the events I have described, after a certain age Japanese children of my era were raised much differently than American children of the same era. In Japan, children belonged to the society, not to their parents. Compared with American families, it seems that Japanese parents maintained a great distance between themselves and their children. In Japan, it is not customary to show affection, especially in public. In America, things are much different. Parents shower their children with physical affection, and it's not unusual to see couples express their affection for each other in public places. I have learned that the physical distance that my parents maintained between themselves and their children was an expression of their love and the end result was a deep, mutual love.

I don't know which method of child raising is better — the Japanese way or the American way. I believe that a balance of physical contact and physical distance is ideal.

There also needs to be an ideal balance between praising and scolding, love and discipline. This belief is reflected in the way that I run Nippon Kan. I don't give many words of appreciation or praise to the people who help me run the *dojo*. I understand how much they do for the organization, and I appreciate their efforts, but — in keeping with my Japanese background — I don't express gratitude by showering them with praise. You won't often find me thanking any of my assistants by saying: "You know, you've provided a great deal of help to our organization. You handle things with great skill and incredible efficiency. I really appreciate your time and assistance." Perhaps they would like to hear such words of praise, but that's simply not the way I learned to express gratitude; it wouldn't be me.

As a non-profit organization, Nippon Kan relies heavily on the voluntary support of its members. Of course, I am fully aware of the work my students do and of their value to the *dojo*. And they understand that their efforts are part of their training.

A few people have left my *dojo* saying, "You're too Japanese for me. This is America." Yes, this is America, but I was born and raised in Japan, and my background is reflected in the way that I live and teach. Nippon Kan is a place where students can achieve whatever goals they set for themselves; it's also a place for them to learn from one another. The *dojo* attracts students from many countries, and in that sense it is borderless. The fact that I'm Japanese or that most of my students are American or that other students come from other countries doesn't matter. When you look at things from a global perspective, a nationalistic perspective seems small-minded.

And so I remain: "Gaku Homma: Race — Mongolian; Nationality — Japanese; Sex — male; Occupation — martial artist." Inside my *dojo*, each student is unique and I am but one of many human exhibits. Students are free to learn from each other and, in doing so, about themselves. In my opinion, this is what a *dojo* is about. What I have told you about my childhood and my views on martial arts are offered as "food for thought." As a martial arts instructor, one of my responsibilities is to provide my students with examples, stories, and opinions, which is one of the reasons I wrote this book. Now let's return to the children's Aikido class.

KIDS WILL BE ... PUPPIES

Before the children's class begins at Nippon Kan, the students enjoy a few minutes of free time on the mat. It's interesting to watch them play in a situation that is not rigidly structured. They run around with each other like a bunch of puppies. If you look closely at them, you discover something interesting. The younger children are constantly "challenging" the older students; they especially challenge the older students who are the natural leaders. By "challenge" I don't mean the kind of serious kind of confrontation you see on TV or in movies. There's no punching or kicking. They just grab and tackle and try to get on top. Some of the smaller children jump on the leader's back, hang from his arms, and so on. Occasionally, the younger students mimic what they've seen on TV — they assume fighting stances and scream — but when they actually attack, they don't punch or kick. Instead, they grab and tackle like the rest of the children.

It seems that usually the children instinctively know what actions are acceptable. They are able to distinguish between the fantasy world they see on television and the real world that they live in. The information they have gathered watching their cartoon, television, and movie heroes makes up their fantasy world; the information they have received from their parents, other family members, and teachers, makes up their real world. They have learned through their "real world" lessons that they shouldn't punch or kick other children. When they imitate their heroes with fighting stances and screams, they are performing in their fantasy world, but when they actually "attack" the older children, they become frolicking puppies.

It is very important for children to be able to distinguish between fantasy and reality. There are children who cannot tell the two worlds apart. This is why I have been stressing that children should never be taught to use punches and kicks when dealing with others or solving problems.

Even martial art tournaments with strict regulations are basically encouraging children to punch and kick each other. If you encourage children to punch and kick, even in a controlled tournament, they will believe that punching and kicking are acceptable when dealing with other people.

When the children play before Aikido class begins, the older leaders are always careful not to get too rough with their young attackers — no matter how many youngsters are on top of them. The leaders free themselves by grabbing the young students or by picking them up by their belts. Before long, everybody is out of breath.

When the children play, all of them follow a set of unwritten rules. They don't need to discuss what's allowed and what's not; it's understood. Occasionally, a new student will come to class and break one of the unwritten rules, perhaps by actually trying to kick one of the leaders. Such an action warrants a stern look, perhaps a verbal warning. If this kind of behavior persists, the older students begin to ignore the student who is breaking the rules. It reminds me of the way a dog treats her puppies. When a puppy gets too excited or too rough, the mother dog snaps at it and forces it away from the rest of the litter. The puppy looks sad and walks away. But before long, he/she is back romping with the rest of the group.

When a young student breaks the rules, the student is gently pushed away from the group. But soon the student is back — following the rules this time. Unacceptable behavior is not tolerated. When a new student continues to break the rules, the leader must eventually intervene. When this happens, the other students lose some of their play time, and they make it clear to the offender that such behavior isn't tolerated. Most new students quickly learn to blend in with the group and become one of the "puppies."

The younger students learn from this type of experience. After a few years they become the leaders of the group and they handle their juniors as they were handled — gently. This tradition is handed down from the older students to the younger students year after year. This is one of the lessons that they can draw from when they grow up and are faced with real-life problems. The pre-class play session teaches children to solve basic problems in a positive way, to resolve conflicts in a way that is acceptable to everybody.

I consider the emphasis of natural childlike behaviors to be of utmost importance in Aikido classes. Our classes do not include training in destructive force such as punching and kicking, nor do we break bricks or boards. We do not hold tournaments, because I believe tournaments reinforce destructive behavior and competition. I feel it is very important to reinforce positive, natural behavior, and to try to negate the negative influences some martial arts, especially those portrayed in the movies, can have on children.

Once I observed a children's class at a martial arts *dojo* where punching and kicking were stressed. Before the class began, the children were playing, running around, and rolling on top of one another much as they do at my *dojo.* Nobody made fists, threw punches, or kicked. When class began, the students practiced punches and kicks with dramatically changed personalities. As I observed this, I realized that all the rules that the children naturally followed when they played together were completely ignored during the class. Even worse, some of the actions that weren't allowed when they played together — punching and kicking — were encouraged during class.

In the world of children, new children are usually welcomed at once. An experienced student who extends his hand to the new student reflects the true spirit of children. At Nippon Kan, we constantly encourage the continuing students to make new students feel welcome. Of course, we've had new students who weren't able to blend in with the continuing students. Often, we find that these students — and their parents — have developed an image of martial arts based on television and movies that they cannot separate from the real world. They have failed to realize that when someone lands a punch, someone else usually gets hurt. This type of student doesn't understand what it's like to be on the receiving end of a punch or kick.

I have told you about the training I received as a member of my neighborhood group. Much of what I learned involved getting along with other children. Today's children don't often get to interact with as many other kids their age. Consequently, they miss out on a lot of social training. I think it is good that many parents have turned to martial arts to help their children develop discipline. But it's very important for parents to realize that the martial art they choose for their children can have a big impact on how their children act. Part of being a child is learning to distinguish between acceptable and unacceptable behavior, between reality and fantasy. Parents who choose a martial art in which kicking and punching are emphasized will likely have children who use "kick and punch" strategies when confronted with problems.

CHILDREN AVOID COLLISIONS

After the students in our children's class have had a few minutes to acquaint themselves with each other and to play freely on the mat, the instructors direct them to run around on the mat. The students begin to run in every direction. You might think that a group of children running helter-skelter in a relatively small area would result in a lot of collisions. But this isn't the case. Occasionally, a student doesn't pay attention and a collision does occur.

But generally they are happy to dodge each other. These are the natural actions of children; they do them almost unconsciously.

When you think about it, it takes a lot of skill and coordination for the children to avoid colliding with each other. But their actions are totally spontaneous. They would do the same thing in any similar situation — inside or outside Aikido class. Unconsciously, children avoid collisions. They dodge their fellow students; they jump over or around obstacles in their path. Children learn from a very early age that it is not a good idea to challenge something that is in their way. They quickly understand that it is best to get out of the way of an oncoming car, bicycle, or their big brother. Similarly, it would never occur to someone who teaches small children to tell a child to face down a person, bike, or car and try to destroy them in self-defense.

As we grow older, we are often taught to "take the bull by the horns" when confronted with a problem. We learn to "fight fire with fire," to react to a problem or an adversary by forcibly defending our own position. This kind of approach may provide momentary successes, but in the long run I think people who constantly butt heads with obstacles and other people wind up with stress-related problems.

We have the children run to show them that it is important to view obstacles not as enemies, but as something one can work in harmony with to overcome. Discussion, persuasion, compromise, and cooperation are techniques that lead to the best solutions. In adult classes, people walk to demonstrate the same thing. For example, when two people approach each other from opposite directions in a crowded area, they naturally adjust their direction to avoid a collision. It doesn't require a set of rules, a formal discussion, or a retreat by either person. Without speaking, they move out of each other's way.

It is also important for children to learn that "peak performance" isn't the goal of martial arts practice. It doesn't matter whether children learn techniques that will help them win tournaments or subdue their friends and enemies. What they need to learn are conflict resolution techniques. Skills that they can use in their everyday lives.

When children study a martial art, they should be taught that the person they are practicing with is not an enemy but a friend.

If children practice with "opponents" or "enemies," during class, they learn to treat other people as adversaries. If they practice with "partners," they learn to treat other people as friends.

Many martial arts *dojos* cite "self-defense" as one of the skills they teach. Often, *dojos* that emphasize self-defense techniques also teach that a large component of good *defense* is good *offense*. The message is that if someone attacks you, it's okay to attack them back. A common theme in Western movies illustrates this point and shows where it can lead: A group of bad guys show up in a town of good people. Their unlawful behavior finally pushes the good guys to the limit and they begin to fight for their rights. The bad guys — now under attack from the good guys — defend themselves. After all, they are being attacked. If it's okay for someone who is being attacked to resort to offensive techniques in the name of self defense, then the outlaws are justified in "defending" themselves against the good guys. This is why I believe that teaching fighting skills as a method of self-defense is a negative, destructive approach: it is often unclear in a conflict who the "good" guy is. The best method of self defense is to avoid collisions.

There is an old story told in Japan about lanterns. A lantern at night is useful to light the area around your feet so you can see where you are going.

"One night to my surprise," begins a storyteller, "a blind man walked by me carrying a lantern. "Why are you walking with a lantern?" I asked. "You cannot see." The blind man answered, "So that others do not run into me." Later, in the dark on a moonless night, I saw two lanterns toppled over and burning, casting shadows on two travelers arguing. "Didn't you see my lantern?" shouted one at the other. "Didn't you see *mine?*" said the other. I realized then that neither man could see."

The moral of the story is that a tool is only as useful as the circumstances in which it is used.

This parable holds true if you replace the lanterns with self-defense skills. True self-defense shines a light around your feet, so that you will be able to proceed each day without hitting or tripping on something. Avoiding collisions, whether they are with another person or an object is a true form of self-defense. Children in the *dojo* run around without colliding with one another because each of them carries a lantern within. Children have that capacity from the time when they are very small. Teaching children who are naturally considerate of others to practice punching and kicking is like blindfolding them, extinguishing their lanterns, and telling them to walk.

When it's time for children's class to begin, the teachers instruct the students to "Line up!" If a child takes too long to line up, teachers tell the kids to start again by running around the *dojo* once and then lining up quickly. It soon becomes apparent if any one child in particular is holding up the class. Usually the other children help the child unaware of the need to hurry to line up. Unless the case is severe I advise my instructors not to interfere but to let the children discover how they are to line up for themselves. The children form lines according to their age and experience and face the front of the *dojo*. They sit in a traditional Japanese position called *seiza*. Their knees are bent underneath them, slightly apart, and they sit on their heels. Many martial art *dojos* require students to sit in this position, but originally it was limited to a handful of Japanese martial arts. In martial art training — where the ability to respond quickly to an attack is considered essential — *seiza* is the least defensible position. Among other things, this posture expresses submission to authority. In martial arts classes, it also expresses respect for the traditional spirit of the *dojo*.

This posture of non-violence reaffirms Aikido's non-confrontational approach. In feudal Japan, a man who wished to meet with people in power wore a long *hakama* (baggy, skirt-like pants often worn by the *samurai*) that was at least four feet longer than his legs. A man who wore a *hakama* and sat in *seiza* showed that he did not intend to fight. Sometimes television shows and movies have scenes in which someone sits in an aggressive *seiza* position, with their knees far apart, fists on knees, and shoulders raised. The jaw muscles are tight, the face is stern. This is Hollywood; not *seiza*. As I explained earlier, sitting in *seiza* is an expression of non-aggression. To put on an aggressive face while sitting in *seiza* is a contradiction. In feudal Japan, an aggressive *seiza* position would have resulted in a quick beheading.

In addition to its symbolic meaning, sitting in *seiza* has other significance. On a purely physical level, it's a good way to maintain flexible knees. These days, most people sit on chairs or couches. In a normal sitting position, the knees are bent at a ninety-degree angle, which isn't nearly as far as they are capable of bending. People who never stretch their legs end up with stiff joints, which — in turn — are easily injured. Many adults with weak and injured knees are forced to use knee supports when they exercise. In order to avoid stiff and injured knees, Aikido practice includes sitting in the *seiza* position.

Traditionally, Japanese have not suffered from the knee problems that beset many Westerners. Because sitting in *seiza* has traditionally been a common practice, the knees of Japanese people retained their natural flexibility. However, Western customs are replacing many Japanese traditions, and I'm afraid that as a result, an increasing number of Japanese people will be forced to wear knee supports.

Anyway, unlike adult students, most children can sit comfortably in *seiza* position. After bowing to begin class, the students sit with their shoulders relaxed and fingers softly opened on their knees. Their chins are pulled in slightly to keep their backs straight.

It is better for children to learn to maintain a calm, gentle appearance than to learn how to look mean and aggressive. A child who is not aggressive does not make enemies. Some martial art *dojos* teach children how to make fists, assume aggressive stances, and to put on mean faces. Are these the kinds of things children should learn? I don't think so.

After the students have lined up and are sitting in *seiza*, everyone — students and instructors — bows to the front of the *dojo*. The lead instructor then turns to face the class, and the students and instructor bow to each other. I will explain the significance of bowing later. A set of stretching exercises follows.

LEARNING ABOUT LIMITS

During the stretching exercises, the kids count. *"Ichi, Ni, San, Shi, Go!"* (sounds like "each, knee, san, she, go). "One, Two, Three, Four, Five!" Usually, we count in Japanese. Sometimes we use English; other times we use different languages. We only use the numbers from one to five, so it's not too difficult for the students. The language they use doesn't matter; the important lesson is that movements are more powerful when they are accompanied by a strong voice.

Your voice is a reflection of your intentions. You do what you tell yourself to do. If you tell yourself, "It's time to eat," you will take action and find something to eat. If you wait around for somebody to tell you to eat, you're likely to get hungry and weak. The same principal applies to Aikido students. A student with a faint voice often moves weakly, unsurely. Developing a strong voice helps a child to develop strong movements.

In some *dojos*, students stretch silently while the instructor shouts out the count. In other *dojos*, the instructor stretches on the count of "One." The students follow and count, "One." Then it's the instructor's turn to lead, "Two!" Then it's the students' turn, "Two." In both of these cases, the students' actions are controlled by the instructor. The students are followers, not initiators. They are not controlling their own actions. At Nippon Kan, students stretch to the rhythm of their own voice, and by doing so, they learn that they control their own actions. They also develop a strong, positive voice, which is useful not only for martial art applications but in daily life as well. By learning to use voice and therefore breathing in a powerful manner, children can learn to express themselves with greater confidence. This kind of training can lead to the positive, outgoing attitudes children need to take their own initiative. Initiatives are strong and positive when they are the result of blending will and intentions, voice and physical movements.

The stretching exercises are accompanied by a strong voice and exhalation. Breathing is really quite interesting. People can exhale — with voice — for a minute or more. When it's time to inhale, it only takes a few seconds to refill the lungs with air. I don't mean to downplay inhaling (it is quite important!), but in Aikido class, we focus more on exhaling — which is a form of positive self-expression.When we are surprised, scared, or nervous we tend to inhale or hold our breath. When we are calm and moving with direction, our breathing (especially exhalations) is deep.

Children who are overly shy, who don't show much initiative, tend to have a rapid, shallow breath. I have found that in many instances, children who behave like this have been told,

"Keep quiet" or "You're too noisy" excessively at home. To reverse these children's tendency to withdraw, it is best to focus their training on action accompanied by a strong voice, where exhaling is emphasized.

In Aikido class, children learn to stretch their muscles — a little further than their muscles normally stretch — while exhaling in a loud voice. At first, when they reach their limit and they start to feel a little bit of pain in the muscles they are stretching, their voices become high-pitched. But they don't stop at that point. We encourage them to stretch — gently — just a little further, to push their bodies a little beyond what they think their limits are.

Many children today seem to have tight joints and stiff bodies. I have seen many new students who were barely able to sit crosslegged on the mat. Their legs and their backs are so tight, they have to prop themselves up with their hands to avoid falling over backward. Their faces show their discomfort. They may be young, but they are much stiffer than the senior citizens who attend our weekly meditation class. When I see stiff, young students, it makes me wonder what they do at school and at home. A single Aikido class lasts an hour. That's not enough time to make up for an inactive lifestyle.

Children's stiffness is a reflection of the kind of lives they lead. They spend more time watching television and playing video games — passive exercises— than they do playing, chasing each other around, and wrestling with their playmates. These are the kind of natural activities that keep children limber. Watching television is a way for children to get information, but it doesn't teach them to take action. When children are inactive, they begin to lose the natural balance between body and mind. And its not just bodies that become stiff. Some children of the television age can't distinguish between the fantasy world they see on TV and the real world in which they live. They see so much violence on television that violence and pain have no real meaning for them. They begin to see other people as television characters, and treat them as though they have no real feelings of their own.

The stretching exercises at the beginning of class help children understand what it feels like to live in the real world. As they stretch their muscles and exercise their voices, they learn what it feels like to push their bodies to the limit. They learn to balance the information that television supplies to their minds with the experience that stretching supplies to their bodies. Over time, children learn how far they can stretch their bodies before they begin to feel a little bit of pain. They need to learn to distinguish the pain that results in injury, from the kind of pain that tells them where their limits are. Normally children who learn what pain feels like are careful not to inflict pain on others.

Sometimes, martial art *dojos* teach their students to stretch in pairs. One person applies pressure to stretch the other. At Nippon Kan we do not stretch in pairs because it's only natural to react to pressure applied by someone else by getting tense. The person who's being stretched often resists when pushed to the limit. It's impossible for the person who is applying the pressure to know what the other person is feeling.

I feel it is better for students to push themselves, for only they know their true limits.

Stretching exercises teach children how to find their limits, to learn what pain feels like, and to deal with pain. These are lessons that also help them get along with other children. Of course, one of the purely physical benefits of the stretching exercises is a more limber body.

Little by little, after many repetitions, the stretching exercises teach children how to keep their bodies in good working condition. The pain the students feel in stretch exercises is a tool to work with in learning to control and maintain their bodies. A thorough set of stretching exercises is followed by a set of Aikido-specific exercises. (See Part 2 for more information about stretching exercises.)

MOVING NATURALLY

A set of Aikido exercises follows the stretching exercises described in the previous section. The Aikido exercises give the students a chance to loosen up their bodies before they divide into pairs and begin working on Aikido techniques. These exercises include twisting and stretching the wrists and a few basic foot movements. Each of the Aikido-specific exercises is part of an Aikido technique.

Rather than focus now on the mechanics of the Aikido exercises, I would like to take a look at the purpose of these exercises. By doing them before each class, the students get a chance to work on the techniques they will later practice in pairs. Some martial arts use practice techniques that require students to respond to punches and kicks thrown by imaginary enemies. This isn't the case during Aikido practice. Aikido students practice techniques by working in pairs; not alone. The Aikido-specific warmup exercises help students develop the ability to focus their attention and their energy and to respond calmly to anything that happens. These exercises help students develop an awareness of the relationship between their intentions and their physical actions — that is, between their minds and their bodies.

Some Aikido *dojos* attribute the harmony of mind and body to the discovery of *ki*. They teach that understanding *ki* is the goal of Aikido practice. The issue here is not *ki* itself, but the method widely thought of as the training of *ki*. At Nippon Kan, the first thing that we tell new students is that there's nothing mysterious about Aikido or *ki*. The elusive *ki* that other *dojos* talk about isn't something that you suddenly find outside of yourself, nor is it something that happens after a few hundred dollars worth of lessons. You don't have to pay money; you don't have to have a religious experience to understand *ki*. All you have to do is move and sweat. After many countless hours of moving and sweating, you will discover what you already know: "I am here." What more is there to know?

In children's class, we teach students to move as naturally as possible using the same kind of movements they use every day. If we were to tell them to project their *ki*, they would only become confused. And if we taught them to stand in strange positions and to make strange movements, they wouldn't have much use for Aikido in their day-to-day affairs. When we move our bodies freely, without worry, our mind follows and becomes free and calm. This is a person's natural state. We try to teach the children that it's okay for them to be themselves. I don't see any value in teaching them complicated concepts and difficult movements.I think that *dojos* that try to teach children to develop their *ki* are forcing an adult concept and an adult approach to life on them. Children react spontaneously, naturally when something happens. Children shouldn't be forced to act like adults, and they shouldn't be forced to learn mysterious concepts — like *ki*.

During the wrist-stretching exercises that we do at the beginning of the children's class, the instructor will often stop and check a student's stability by applying a slight push to the student's hands. The children react in one of three ways: one type collapses at the elbows as soon as pressure is applied to the hands; the second type overreacts in anticipation of the push and falls forward even before pressure is applied; and the third type gets very stiff and is easily pushed backwards. The reactions are the same when this technique is used with adult students. All of the reactions are normal. If you think that someone is going to push you, it's only natural for you to react.

Over time the students learn to respond to the instructor's push with equal pressure — and without anticipating. Each time, they improve a little; they become a little more stable. This is what's important. Aikido training provides children with many opportunities to develop themselves. After many repetitions, after many trials and errors and trials and successes, they learn to have confidence in their actions.

One of the footwork exercises children do before class is called "*tenkan-undo*" (body spin exercise). In this exercise, the children take two steps to turn 180⁻ to see what's behind them. The footwork is quite easy and even new students are quickly able to master it. Soon, they are having fun with the exercise, turning from front to back, stepping lightly, almost skipping. These are the natural motions of a child. Next, I bring out a small wooden sword and tell them in a loud voice, "We're going to continue practicing the same footwork, except that this time I'm going to swing this sword at you! Do exactly the same move; use the same steps to get out of the way."

As soon as they see me holding a sword, some of the children start to become tense; some hold their breath. Sadly enough, most children know what swords are. After practicing with the wooden sword, I replace it with another, longer wooden sword, saying. "Now, I'll strike you with this long sword!" By this time, some children have been fascinated into motionlessness; others are still skipping as they were before I introduced the sword.

The students who freeze up know that they are not in any danger of actually being hit. Yet they focus on the sword to the exclusion of everything else — including the footwork that was so easy a few minutes before. My point is that, these children are reacting to a wooden sword because of what they've read in books or seen on television, in movies or around their neighbor hood. The children who aren't bothered by the presence of the wooden sword continue to move naturally — like children.

With practice, children learn to stay calm in this situation. They learn that they can easily get out of the way when something is moving toward them — no matter what the oncoming force is. Sometimes a great deal of patience is required. After all, children spend only an hour each week in Aikido class. Habits that have developed over many years can't be changed overnight. Eventually, children develop confidence in their actions. When this happens, their movements become graceful and effortless — which is the way children naturally move when they are playing and having fun.

GOING WITH THE FLOW

A set of rolling/falling exercises follows the Aikido-specific exercises discussed in the previous section. Unlike adults, who often have difficulty doing *ukemi* (rolling to protect one's body) exercises, children learn them quickly. The children have been walking for quite some time by the time they enroll in Aikido class. Still, they have a lot of fun rolling around on the mat. There is about 1700 square feet of mat space, and the children roll from one corner along all four sides many times at a surprisingly fast pace. They do about a dozen forward rolls and a dozen backward rolls before returning to the starting corner. This important movement of *ukemi* or rolling, or tumbling in general, is one unique feature of Aikido training. The human body has evolved to enable us to walk on only two of our four limbs. However, every infant goes through a crawling stage, and before that we all spent time curled up in the womb. For the children in Aikido class, the falling down exercises are much like the rolling and crawling they did when they were a bit younger.

Learning to fall down without getting injured is a key concept in Aikido; and the way in which falling down is perceived is very important to understanding Aikido. In most martial arts, falling down is equated with losing. The very word — "down" — has generally negative connotations. "I'm feeling down today. My computer is down. The economy is down. The contestant was knocked down."

Over the years we learn to stay upright. By the time we become adults, falling down in general is avoided. You will find this emphasis on staying vertical in many martial art *dojos*. Many *dojos* have hard floors, which punish those who fall. In tournaments, when one opponent falls down, the other opponent receives points. For these reasons, many martial art *dojos* that teach kicking and punching techniques don't teach falling techniques at all. For children studying these disciplines the joy in the childhood play of rolling around and tumbling with friends is no longer acceptable but taboo. What happened to the movements these children grew up with?

Judo, although practiced on a mat like Aikido, is another martial art that attaches a stigma to falling. In Judo, the object is to throw your opponent. Getting thrown is the worst thing that can happen to you. Therefore, when a Judo practitioner is about to be thrown, he hangs on as tight as he can hoping at least to drag his opponent down with him. Even after both practitioners hit the floor the two continue to struggle until one side gives up. This kind of practice — with many hard falls — has a risk of neck and shoulder injuries.

Students who learn to fear and avoid falling down get stiff and awkward when they do have to fall. As a result, they are more likely to get injured than students who learn to relax and "go with the flow" when headed for the floor.

Aikido students learn to fall down without getting injured. They learn that falling down is a part of practice, and that it does not have the negative connotations we usually associate with it. They learn to react to falling with the kind of natural, relaxed rolling motions that they have been doing in play for years.

In Aikido, there are no winners or losers; only partners. Everybody takes turns falling down. One person throws; the other person falls. Then they switch. The person who did the throwing now does the falling, and vice versa. Practice is always balanced in this way. Even though one person is the initiator and one person is the defender, by switching back and forth, everybody learns both sides. The one who initiates is not an enemy to the person dealing with their force. Neither side is the good side or the bad side. For every ten minutes the children practice throwing, they also practice ten minutes of falling.

The partner who is practicing his or her falling has to learn to judge the surrounding area and find the safest place, time and direction to take his or her roll. *Ukemi* practice is learning to fall naturally, and is not concerned with winning and losing. We don't take rolls because our partners force us with a throw. Instead we learn to sense what our partners want to do and in which direction, and take their lead finishing the technique with a roll. You will notice that to practice learning this flow, the partner who initiates the movements is cooperative, and takes his or her roll easily without resisting.

Suppose you are walking in a park at night, and you trip on a tree stump. Do you kick the stump in return? Do you try to hold on to the stump in order not to fall? In Aikido, the solution would be first to sense the stump and not trip, or if you started to lose your balance, to roll out of the situation as if nothing drastic had gotten in your path.

Let's look at a real-life example of how knowing how to fall can come in handy. Have you ever seen somebody trip and fall down? Usually, a person who is about to fall does everything possible to avoid falling. Often, by the time the person falls, the body is in an awkward position. Under these circumstances, a simple fall can lead to serious injury. Older people can break wrists or hips when they fall down unexpectedly because they haven't fallen in years and have forgotten how to "roll with it." In Aikido, falling and rolling are a very important part of practice. One hope is that by learning to fall in class, students will avoid injury if they are forced to fall outside of class.

In addition to protecting the children's bodies from falling-related injuries, *ukemi* exercises have other benefits. Doing back rolls (backward *ukemi*) — rocking forward and backward along the back — places a little bit of rolling pressure along the spine. Stomach and back muscles tighten and relax rhythmically; the pressure of the lower back against the mat provides a gentle massage; the rubbing action of the heavy fabric of the *keiko-gi* (practice uniform) against the body has the same effect as the centuries-old Oriental healing method called *kampu masatsu,* or rubbing with a dry cloth. It stimulates tiny blood lines on or just beneath the skin. By coordinating your breathing with the rolling, the entire body participates.

Rolling forward, relaxing briefly, then rolling backward teaches the children to balance rest with action, relaxing and extending. Moving and stopping are two actions that we perform every day, and the simplified version of the movements practiced in backward *ukemi* help train us to be able to separate the two distinctly. A child who is about to give a recital will often get overly nervous, and be unable to act calmly when needed. It's not much use telling him or her to relax, as we all know it can be very difficult to control ourselves under stressful circumstances. Being able to extend and relax yourself at will is not something you can easily order yourself to do, but is something you can train yourself to become more and more aware of. Your mind needs to be focused on what your body is doing. You can achieve this focus by practicing movements as simple as those practiced in backward *ukemi.* Focusing on harmonizing body movement, mind, and breathing can help us to learn to relax and extend ourselves appropriately.

Ukemi practice is not an indication of defeat by an opponent. It is not running away, it is a very important movement of human beings. Sensing a partners' movements and falling in accordance with his or her technique, from one's own will, is a valuable skill. Refining this ability, using it for self protection and for fun, are the reasons for *ukemi* in Aikido.

"REI" IS A REFLECTION OF YOURSELF

After *ukemi* exercises, the students are ready to start practicing Aikido techniques. But before they begin, there's one last — and very important — task, one that is practiced in almost all Japanese martial art classes. In Aikido, it's called *"rei."*

Some time ago, I looked up *"rei"* in a Japanese-English dictionary. The English synonyms included: "bow," "etiquette," "salutation," "thanks," and "reward." None of these words accurately describe what *"rei"* means to a Japanese person. In one Japanese dictionary, *"rei"* is defined as follows:

"The actions people must follow when interacting with others so that social order is maintained; a ceremonial gesture used to express respect to others; gifts or words to carry feeling of appreciation to others."

Although it is only a three-letter word, the concept of *rei* is very important in Japanese culture.

The most literal English interpretation of *rei* is to bow — the same action that instructors and students perform when they enter the *dojo*, when they begin practice, before and after they practice with each other, and at the end of class. However, instead of using the word "bow" in this chapter, I will use the original Japanese term, which has a much deeper and broader meaning.

I don't spend a lot of time explaining the many meanings of *rei* to the children. It wouldn't mean much to them if I explained in detail how the practice of *rei* is a sign of respect in Japanese culture. When children feel respect for somebody, it shows in their actions. It would be very strange if a five or six year-old child showed appreciation by sitting in *seiza* and bowing deeply.

For American children, it is natural to show respect for someone by saying, "Hi," by nodding, or by shaking hands. It's not necessary for them to act like a Japanese person when they want to show their respect. So, at Nippon Kan, children perform *rei* to signal the end of one activity and the beginning of another. When practiced like this, *rei* performs the same function in Aikido that a period (.) performs for a written sentence: It marks the end of one sentence and signals the beginning of another.

Somebody might argue that *rei* is not necessary; that you can begin and end things without bowing. However, as I have said many times in previous chapters, one of the key concepts of Aikido is that physical action is necessary to reinforce what is going on in our mind. Sometimes, it's impossible to tell what a child is thinking, especially if the child isn't doing anything.

However, when children practice *rei*, it is clear that their minds are in control of their bodies. Each time a child sits in *seiza* and bows, it marks a transition.

Some parents are at first uncomfortable with the practice of *rei*. Some request that their children be excused from bowing to the front of the *dojo*, where a picture of the founder of Aikido hangs. They get the impression that *rei* is some sort of religious practice. When this happens, I explain that *rei* has nothing to do with religion. If they still feel uncomfortable about it, I tell them that it's not mandatory.

I have had some students from the Middle East whose cultural background prevented them from sitting in *seiza* and bowing to other people. At first they were uncomfortable and hesitant when it was time to perform *rei*. But after a while, they developed their own way of performing *rei*. Their technique was a little different than other students, but the meaning behind it was the same. The essence of *rei* is not found in the physical action of bowing. It's the meaning behind the action that's important. However, as I mentioned earlier, during children's class we don't dwell on the philosophical significance of *rei*.

How useful is it to teach American children to kneel and bow deeply when they feel respect for somebody or something? It would be silly for an American child to bow to every adult. Besides, when someone shows respect for another person, the gesture should be one that the receiver of the gesture understands. Ultimately, by showing respect for others, children learn to respect themselves. When someone is happy, everything is a source of joy and everything is worthy of respect. Such a person understands the meaning of the Japanese word *Okagesamade,* which means "for blessings extended toward me." When a person is thankful for life, everything and everybody is deserving of thanks.

In Japan, *rei* is practiced every day in both personal and professional relationships. For example, members of athletic teams remove their hats and bow to the field or the court before entering and before leaving. This is not a religious action, and it is not directed toward any particular individual. The athletes are simply bowing to the field or court to show their respect. It is an action of humility that says, *"Okagesamade,* we are able to practice today."

One of the things I enjoy most about teaching children is watching them express *rei*. I remember one occasion when a young student brought me a hand-drawn birthday card. He shyly handed the card to me after the class, and his feelings were obvious even though he didn't say anything. Another time, a student ran out of the *dojo* after his class. A few seconds later, he ran back and gave me a big hug saying, "Thank you, Sensei!" These actions reflected the essence of *rei*.

"REI" IS EASILY MISUNDERSTOOD

I would like to share with you a story about the practice of *rei* that shows how it is often misunderstood. A few years ago, I was invited to an Aikido *dojo* in another state to teach at a seminar. After I had finished teaching a class, a young student brought me a glass of water; another brought me a towel. I said, "Thank you," and asked, "Why did you offer me such nice things?" "Because you are *Sensei*," they answered. It was nice to be the receiver of such respect.

Later that day, one of my assistants taught a class. About ten minutes before the class ended, I went to the *dojo* to observe. After the class ended, the same students brought me a glass of water and a towel. I think you can see the problem here. These children were instructed to bring water and a towel to me because I was "*Sensei*." Even though my assistant had taught the afternoon class and was the one who had earned some water and a towel, the children brought them to me. This kind of superficial *rei* is common and shows how the concept is often misunderstood.

Nippon Kan attracts many students who have practiced martial arts at other *dojos*. Such new students often perform the rituals they have learned in other *dojos*. Some hold their fists tightly, stand straight up and stiff, bow mechanically, and shout "*Ossu!*" You may think that all Japanese students behave like this in a martial arts class, but this is not the case at all. This type of behavior is limited to a particular style of martial art school, and it's usually limited to college-age students. If a Japanese person were to say "*Ossu,*" under normal circumstances — on the job, for example — it would be a clear sign that the person wasn't ready for the adult world. No employer would be impressed by an employee who bowed and said *"Ossu!"*

Some time ago, I attended a dinner party. During the evening, the host told me his son was practicing martial arts and wanted to demonstrate what he had learned. The boy got ready to perform a *"kata,"* (a series of stylized offensive and defensive motions) beginning with *"Ossu!"* He wore an oversized uniform, clenched his fists tightly, and stiffly went through the movements of the *kata*. His father was obviously proud. I smiled throughout the demonstration. When it was over, I told the boy that he was very good. Then I asked him, "What does *'Ossu'* mean?" "It is a respectful bow," he answered. "I see," I said.

In Japan, *Ossu* has come to mean something like, "How's it going?" But it has never been a formal way to greet anybody. If you study the origin of the word *Ossu*, you'll find that the two *Kanji* characters that make up the written word mean "push" and "patience." Literally, it means "to be patient and to be patient some more." It became popular among college students after World War II and it was also adopted by martial art *dojos* that emphasized punching and kicking.

Why did it become popular at martial arts *dojos*? Not because it implied that the students would react patiently if attacked. Just the opposite. During the *samurai* period, anyone caught practicing a martial art who was not a member of the *samurai* class was put to death. The martial philosophy behind saying *"Ossu"* was developed by the non-*samurai* class of people to protect themselves from the violent predators of the era. *Ossu* became an expression of patience against oppression and of self sacrificing retaliation against the oppression. This is the tradition that was inherited by post-World War II martial arts students. Saying *"Ossu"* implied that no matter what happened to their body — whether it was punched, kicked, stabbed, or shot — they will continue to respond by hitting, kicking, and doing anything possible as long as their bodies could function.

More than anything else, saying *"Ossu"* came to signify tolerance against pain. It became a declaration of the fighting spirit based on self-sacrifice. When you see people demonstrate martial arts that teach this approach, the demonstrators are usually naked from the waist up. Sometimes the demonstrators are pounded with wooden sticks. Other times they break baseball bats with their shins or bricks with their hands. Often they yell, "*Ossu!*" before such demonstrations. It doesn't matter to them that one mistake could lead to a serious injury. Self-sacrifice is the goal. I know many people who have hurt themselves trying to demonstrate their ability to sacrifice their bodies. What's the point?

This approach to fighting was not found among *samurai* warriors. When *samurai* fought *samurai*, there was an accepted code of conduct. A *samurai* had to be prepared to fight at any moment. As a result, they paid close attention to their bodies and their health. Self-sacrifice in training was not considered a virtue. A *samurai* would not risk physical injury by breaking boards or bricks.

Having been raised in Japan, I learned the practice of *rei*, and as a student of Aikido I learned how the practice of *rei* related to a martial art. When I came to the United States, I was in my late 20s and my actions and reactions were fully Japanese. I had no idea how Americans expressed their respect for each other. At first, I had a terrible time standing close to anybody. In Japan I had learned — as everyone learned — to keep my distance from others. Learning to shake hands was a nightmare for me, hugging — which isn't done in public by Japanese people — was even more difficult. But the biggest obstacle I had to overcome was the Japanese custom of not looking at another person's eyes. In Japan, it is considered terrible manners to look someone directly in the eye. I remember being taught to look at a man's necktie during conversation. In America, such behavior makes other people suspicious. A person who can't look another person eye to eye is thought to be hiding something. The point is that no matter how much respect a person has for another person, cultural differences can lead to misunderstanding.

Before two Aikido students practice together, they each sit on their heels, place both hands on the mat with palms down, and with a straight back, they bow deeply to each other as an expression of *rei*. This simple action is an integral part of our training. In contrast to the practice of "*Ossu*," the practice of *rei* helps develop respect for all people. Given this definition, I think it is the martial arts' responsibility to guide our children in the practice of *rei*.

TECHNIQUES OF DESTRUCTION; TECHNIQUES OF HARMONY

Following Aikido exercises and the practice of *ukemi*, we begin *tai-jutsu* training (the practice of techniques). Before I explain the techniques we practice in Aikido class in more detail, there are a few points I want to you to consider. I feel it is very important for parents to examine why they want their children to learn a martial art. One reason can be, as I have said in previous chapters, is that they've seen martial arts heroes on television or in the movies, and want their children to emulate those heroes. In the typical martial arts movie, the bad guys pick on good citizens. They push them around and abuse them until the good guys can no longer take it. Just when their tolerance has reached its limit, a hero shows up to take care of the bad guys. Bruce Lee rips his shirt; the Hulk turns into a green monster; Superman, Rambo, and Zorro come to the rescue; the Karate Kid beats up the Bad Kid.

All heroes are pretty much the same. They punish evil-doers. When they come to the rescue, the audience claps and cheers. People identify with them. These movies make people feel that they too are heroes. And parents, sometimes, imagine their children as potential heroes.

In Hollywood, it's violence that overcomes evil. But the real world is much different than that portrayed in martial arts movies. How often do newspapers run a stories about criminals getting caught, beat up, and captured by a spur-of the moment hero? Not very often. I can't remember ever seeing or hearing about such a story. In the real world, the bad guys are criminals, and their victims are simply victims. Criminals don't look for a hero when they're searching for a victim. They prey on ordinary people. And when they strike, Superman and Bruce Lee don't show up. These heroes exist only in our imaginations.

Many people decide to study martial arts with the illusion that some day they'll have a chance to be a hero. Martial arts magazines are full of ads for deadly weapons that show ordinary people using them to subdue their attackers. Some parents see their children in these ads and imagine them fighting off a gang of bullies using their martial art skills.

Think about it for a moment. Would you really want your child to challenge a group of gang members? A few martial arts classes will not turn a child into a superhero. Martial art training does not make a child invincible. Do you want your child to learn to punch and kick his or her way out of trouble? Children who learn to respond to problems with violence become violent children. Is this what parents want? I don't think so.

Regardless of the circumstances, nobody — and especially children — should resort to violence to solve their problems. Avoiding violence is at the heart of Aikido, as it is in Judo. Neutralizing an attacker — not punishing, injuring, or killing — is the goal of Aikido and Judo techniques. Aikido and Judo students do not respond to attacks with punches and kicks. In other words, Aikido and Judo techniques do not result in intentional injuries. If you can first neutralize an attacker, you can then reason with them.

The Japanese martial arts known as *Budo*, which were developed by the *samurai* class, taught that violence was not an appropriate response to violence. They were developed as a method to control violent situations; to replace violence with non-violence. Avoiding and eliminating violence were the goals. The techniques that were taught and used reflected a non-violent attitude. The *samurai* learned to respond to negative actions with positive actions.

When Aikido students practice Aikido techniques, there are no "good guys" or "bad guys." There are simply two partners working together. Their goal is to master a technique by blending their movements and harmonizing each other's energy. Their goal is not to conquer, but to cooperate. This is why there are no tournaments in Aikido as I teach it.

How can we blend with each other? This is the question that Aikido students are constantly trying to answer. When two students practice a technique, their common goal is to harmonize their movements. When they achieve their goal, both students have succeeded. At Nippon Kan, one of the underlying premises of children's classes is that the primary purpose of martial art training is not self defense that uses violence to combat violence. On the contrary, the goal is to teach children how to get along with each other; how to avoid violence.

Children have naturally competitive spirits. Aikido training provides a way for children to exercise this competitive spirit in positive, socially acceptable ways — with no violence whatever. Aikido practice develops children who do not resort to violence when confronted with a problem; children who are able to get along with other children.

When children practice techniques with each other, the attacks occasionally involve punches and other strikes, but seldom kicks. The punches and strikes provide an opportunity for the children to practice Aikido responses. The emphasis is on the response; not on the attack. The students never respond to a punch or strike with another punch or strike. Aikido students learn that the most important response to a punch is to get out of the way. Once that has been accomplished, they use Aikido techniques to bring the attacker under control. The aggressor is neutralized — not by destructive force, but by calm, circular movements. By practicing smooth, flowing Aikido movements over and over, children learn to move fluidly and to stay calm under pressure.

Aikido students do not learn how to be heroes. Instead, they learn how to make friends and avoid making enemies. A child who is a friend to many and has no enemies will likely be a happy child. If, on top of that, the child is healthy, the child has everything a parent could hope for. It is my hope that Aikido training helps develop this kind of child.

MASTERING THE ESSENTIALS WITH EXPERIENCE

The practice of Aikido techniques begins with finding a partner. Instructors don't tell students who to work with. Each student must find a partner. After all students have formed pairs, they work on a technique together for six or seven minutes. Then they must find new partners. Everybody works with everybody else. Younger students work with older students; large students work with small students; boys work with girls; girls work with boys.

An experienced student who is paired with a beginner takes on the role of the teacher. But a moment later, when the experienced student is paired with an even more experienced student, he or she takes on the role of the student. By practicing with different kinds of partners, students learn to play many roles in a class, and they learn to adjust their actions according to the size, experience, and age of their partner.

The first thing students learn about practicing techniques is to keep their backs straight, relax their shoulders, and keep their hands wide open. We don't teach students to clench their fists or to spread their feet wide apart in martial stances. Aikido students learn to move calmly and naturally. The movements they practice are the natural movements of children.

Here's a quick test you can take that illustrates why Aikido teaches calm, natural movements. Clench your fists tightly and raise your hands above your head as high as possible. Hold this position for a minute or so. Next, do the same thing with your hands open wide as you raise them over your head. Do you notice any difference between the two exercises? Which one felt better? You probably discovered that the clenched-fists exercise was a lot harder and less enjoyable than the open-hand exercise. Which kind of exercise do you think is better for your children? That is why we don't teach children to stiffen their bodies and make fists.

Aikido techniques are divided into four categories: *nage-waza* (throwing), *nage-osae-waza* (throw and hold), *osae-waza* (holding), and *katame-waza* (joint lock). Techniques in each category provide a comfortable and healthy stimulation to muscles and joints. The techniques, as well as the falling and rolling movements, provide students with a completely different set of movements than they would get from sports, most of which are done standing up.

Aikido techniques are characterized by smooth, circular motions that require the joint efforts of both partners. The practice of a technique begins when a student approaches his or her partner. One basic beginning calls for one student to walk up and grab the hand of another student. The student on the receiving end of the grab learns to step aside, grab the partner's hand, and perform a sequence of simple, circular movements that end with the grabber being neutralized. When working in pairs, the students frequently switch roles so that each student becomes familiar with both aspects of a technique.

On one level, students learn to neutralize a person who grabs them, but on another level, they learn something much more basic and much more useful: When something or someone is going to bump into you, get out of the way. The oncoming force could be a child on a bicycle, or a reckless skier. The point is, if something is moving toward you and you sense a problem, make a small step to the side and look at the problem from a different angle. If you stay where you are, you might get hurt. If, for example, the oncoming force were a child on a bicycle, a failure to move could result in two injuries.

Stepping aside has other benefits. By changing your point of view, you can take a look at what's behind you. Something even bigger and more dangerous might be coming up from behind! You never know. The most fundamental lesson here is: First, check your own safety; making sure that you are safe where you stand. After you have assured your safety, escort your partner down to a safe location.

In order to make a proper decision when confronted by a problem, a person must maintain a calm state of mind, but move quickly. Only by practicing the movements over and over can the students arrive at *taitoku* (the mastering of essentials through experience). *Taitoku* happens a little at a time. After many repetitions, students learn to maintain their self-control when confronted with a problem.

I mention *taitoku*, or "mastering through experience," because it is one of the most important aspects of Japanese culture. As I explained earlier, in Japan, distance is maintained between parents and children; and between teachers and students. This is especially true in martial arts *dojos*. This distance is traditionally used by instructors to put promising students through rigorous physical and mental training in order to stimulate the development of *taitoku*. Instructors often throw their best students around the *dojo*. It is very hard work, but the students don't ask many questions and the instructors don't offer much encouragement or advice. When the student is not being thrown around by the instructor, the student practices with the other students. This can go on for a long time. After many falls, an instructor will say to a student, "You seem to have gained some *taitoku,* but it is too early to take it easy." Then the instructor will throw the student around the *dojo* some more.

The few words of encouragement are quickly followed by a lesson in humility. The student quickly remembers what it's like to feel like a beginner. It is tough for students to deal with, but this type of distance is maintained over years of training so that a student doesn't become overconfident. Over time, after many repetitions, a student gains experience and improves. Instructors keep their distance from their students, but not too far. They make it clear to students: "It is only through practice that you can reach *taitoku.*"

Kakari-geiko is a Japanese practice method in which the student is the attacker and the instructor or a senior student is the person being attacked. A single session can go on at a rapid pace for for ten to fifteen minutes. The attacker is thrown, often hard, by the instructor. All the while, the instructor or senior student will criticize the techniques of the attacker, finding fault with the student's technique, attitude, endurance, and so on. When the student begins to get tired, the instructor turns up the pressure. "Is that all you can do? If that's all you can produce, you are better off dead!"

In America, a similar situation would be handled completely differently. During an extremely tough practice, many coaches would offer positive encouragement. "You can do it! You're doing great! Beautiful!" Growing up in Japan, I never heard such praises. But that doesn't mean my instructors didn't encourage me. They did — in the way that I described above. In Japan, instructors emphasizes the distance between teacher and student; in America, instructors often encourage students by removing this distance.

In Japan, *taitoku* occurs only when there is distance between instructor and student; with the student overcoming difficult physical and emotional obstacles. This type of teacher-student relationship is derived from the practice of Zen in Japan.

Traditionally, a master would give a *koan* — a riddle on which to meditate — to a monk in training. When most people think of Zen training, they imagine a peaceful scene with smiling faces. However, in reality, exchanges between teachers and students often developed into shouting matches and occasionally led to fights. Teachers did not praise students. Students did not expect praise for their actions.

This teaching method was adopted by the general public and became the foundation of the Japanese educational system.

You can see evidence of this cultural difference in many situations. For example, at a dinner party in America, it would be acceptable for a guest to say something like, "This is such a delicious dish. Can I have the recipe?" But in Japan, such a scene would never occur. When someone is invited to dinner in Japan, it is not customary to ask for recipes or to ask questions about how the food was prepared. Of course, close friends sometimes exchange such information, but in a formal situation, such questions would be considered impolite.

By asking for the recipe, a guest would be implying that simply by following the recipe, anyone can cook such a wonderful meal. But in Japan, the personal touch is the most important part of cooking — much more important than the recipe and the ingredients. No matter how good the ingredients are, and how great the recipe is, without the chef's personal touch, the food would not have been as good as it was. So, the first respect goes to the person who prepared the food. This situation is another example of how the Japanese believe that you can master a technique only with practice. Experience is the greatest teacher.

By repeating the same movements over and over, children learn Aikido techniques and the philosophy behind them, just as chefs learn how long to cook something without having to look at a recipe. It takes a very long time to master a technique, but each day of practice provides a day's worth of *taitoku*. *Taitoku* is what a student experiences by practicing the same movements over and over. Eventually, a student moves calmly and correctly without thinking.

Because I teach Aikido in the United States, I have slightly modified the traditional Japanese teaching method that I learned as a child, but I have kept the basic principle of maintaining distance. I still believe that this method teaches each student to develop independently and at whatever pace is best for the student. In this sense, Aikido training involves much more than just physical skills; each student learns to handle all kinds of problems. This is a very important aspect of Aikido and one that parents should understand before they enroll their child in a class. Parents who are interested only in the technical aspect of martial arts would be better off enrolling their children in a different kind of class.

In Japan, martial art students learn the spiritual aspect of training through *taitoku*. *Taitoku* begins with practice, and practice begins when one student approaches another. In Aikido training, students learn to ask the questions: "Why am I standing in a place that someone is attacking?" and, "What can I do to get out of this situation?" The emphasis here is placed on finding one's self, then taking the appropriate action. Suppose a student finds himself being held by both wrists. The first question I ask is why would someone end up in this position? It is important to learn that an action always causes a reaction. Using this point of view we understand that a fight or a quarrel always has a cause, and that we can work toward finding a way to remove the cause, sometimes even before conflict begins.

Aikido students learn many techniques, but there are only three basic foot movements for getting out of the way of an oncoming force. Imagine yourself walking along a narrow path. Another person approaches from the opposite direction. You have three options: You can 1) face ahead and step to one side as the person passes you, then step back to the middle of the path and resume walking forward; 2) spin sideways to let the person pass, then continue walking; or 3) swing to the side like an open gate and let the person pass, then continue walking in your original direction.

In Japan, we use the expression, "yielding the way." When you encounter a person while walking on a narrow mountain road, it is natural to step aside, maybe a little bit into the bushes, to let the person pass. Aikido's basic foot movements are indeed a method for "yielding the way." These movements are not meant to defeat or destroy an oncoming force. If you meet a peron on a narrow path, you also have the option to aggressively assert your position, to attack the oncoming person, to injure the person, and then continue on your way. Most people don't want to solve their problems so violently.

The question of whether the traditional method of teaching *taitoku* is good or bad is not the issue here. What is important is to offer our children training that will give them choices in how they respond to situations that come up in every day life. I feel it is important for children to learn to think for themselves and take action for themselves. This is simply one training method that allows children to develop these important skills.

A FAST-FORWARD LOOK AT AN AIKIDO CLASS

Now that I've explained the background of the elements of an Aikido class, let's take a fast-forward look at a class from beginning to end.

Before the class begins, the children start to line up. The lines aren't very straight or balanced. In some places, children are bunched together. In other places, they are spread out. Some are wearing workout uniforms; others are in T-shirts. There are children with short hair, long hair, pony tails, and pig tails. One child's hair is half-combed, half standing on end. Another boy's hair is standing at attention, and it shines from lots of mousse. One boy is still wearing socks, the rest are barefoot. One girl's uniform is inside out. One child runs in late, but he still has to sit next to his favorite classmate. He squeezes into a small space between two other students. Meanwhile, the instructor is shouting, "Line up!" One student is sitting a few steps in front of everyone else, so everybody moves once again. One of the older students guides a new student into place by waving his hand. After some time and effort, the students are sitting in a straight line, more or less.

Good. Oops! One student is already burying his face in the mat, even though it's not yet time to bow. When it is time to bow to the front, another boy gets up and walks to the lobby, where his father tightens the boy's belt. "*Rei*," says everyone — more or less at the same time — to the front. Then they say, "*Onegai shimasu!*" (a Japanese phrase used widely, in this case meaning "Lets practice together") to each other.

To divide the students into two equal lines, the instructor tells them to count aloud, one, two, one, two. One by one, the students begin to count softly, "One," "Two," "One," "Two." "I can't hear you," barks the instructor, raising the energy level of the entire class. "Louder!" "One," "Two," "One," "Two." "I still can't hear you!" "ONE!" "TWO!" "ONE!" "TWO!" "Good. Now, all twos take a step backward." Confusion follows. "No! You're a 'one'. So you don't go back." "What? You want to be next to your friend? She's a 'one;' you're a 'two.' You two are always together, let's try staying apart only for the warm-ups, okay?" One boy, who's from a very large family, is helping some of the younger students find their proper positions; he is used to taking care of younger children.

The warm up exercises start, and the students are doing well, counting as loudly and energetically as they can. While practicing foot movements, one student's foot touches the foot of the student next to him. In an instant, they're playing games with their feet. The instructor soon notices them and tells them to stop playing around. One student moves forward a few feet; the problem is solved. One new student can't figure out what to do, and stands without moving. An older student tries to help the new student, but pretty soon they're both confused. Still, they're both doing their best to work things out.

Now its time for Aikido exercises. The instructor counts aloud along with the students, but doesn't spend much time correcting mistakes. This job is taken care of by the older students. Generally, the students who know how to do the exercises and techniques try very hard to guide the ones who don't know. After a number of unsuccessful attempts, one new student gives up, runs to the corner of the *dojo*, and sits down. The older student who was trying to help shrugs her shoulders and continues. The instructor also continues, noticing but not stopping the student in the corner.

Next, it's time for rolling exercises. "Smaller students, make small rolls!" shouts the instructor. The children — even the new students — roll with incredible ease and speed. After twelve to fifteen consecutive rolls, the children still aren't dizzy. Or if they are, they don't show it. One student rolls too fast and bumps into another student. The student in front lets the careless roller know that he doesn't appreciate being bumped. Pretty soon, it's apparent that they are not agreeing with each other. Other students are now waiting for the scene to end so they can continue rolling. The instructor doesn't interfere. Instead, one of the older students steps in and resolves the matter. Meanwhile, the student who was sitting in the corner is back, rolling like a champion.

Next it's time to begin practicing Aikido techniques. The instructor demonstrates a technique in front of all the students. After explaining what to do, he says, "Everyone make partners." The students bow, then bounce up and start looking for partners. Some make partners in an instant; obviously they have planned ahead. In one case, three students wind up trying to make partners with each other. They talk a little bit and settle things. One moves on to find a different partner. Pretty soon, most have found partners and are practicing the techniques. A few shy students still haven't made partners and are sitting by themselves. One starts to practice his rolls. An older student invites him to join his group, and he happily joins in. Eventually, everyone finds a partner.

An older student is sitting in front of a young student, helping him tie his belt, which had come untied. The older student is struggling. It's hard to tie someone else's belt, though it's so easy to tie your own.

The instructor shouts, "Change partners!" Everyone says, "Thank you," and begins looking for a new partner. Again, some students are slow to find a partner. If a student is too rough, other students find out quickly. Rough students often have a hard time finding partners. Soon, one pair of students is rolling around on the mat. It doesn't look like they're practicing Aikido techniques. Their belts come loose and their practice uniforms start to fall off. They pause, straighten out their uniforms, and before long they're practicing the techniques correctly.

One pair is having a rough time. The larger student has performed a technique with too much force and too roughly. His partner is obviously unhappy. Several students gather around the pair. A short discussion follows. Soon, they find a solution and everybody resumes practicing.

One very young student is hanging on to an older student, paying no attention to the technique they're supposed to be practicing. Another student runs up to the instructor and whispers something in his ear. "Yes, you can go to the bathroom," responds the instructor. Each child moves freely, one moment playing the part of teacher, then the part of student, then the part of peacemaker, then the part of older brother or sister, and so on. Everybody is constantly making new partners. It is truly interesting to watch children in this environment.

After they finish practicing techniques, it's time for some exercise games. This is the part of class that many students look forward to the most. They do push ups, sit ups, bunny jumps, seal crawls, worm wiggles, wheelbarrows and many other exercises. The instructor doesn't have to say much during this part of class. They know what to do without being told. When the instructor shouts, "Go!" the students take off like race horses. Older students are usually faster than younger ones, but some of the exercises are easier for younger students. Some students have problems with some of the exercises. Some try to cheat; others complain. Students who don't follow the rules must begin again. One young student is having problems with his uniform, which is falling off. Another student runs up to help him. One student who often finishes last is approaching the finish line. The other students are cheering for him. When he finishes, there is loud applause.

A wheelbarrow race begins. The children know that this exercise requires teamwork. They know that the best wheelbarrow teams are the ones in which the partners are about the same size. One student can't find a partner. Others have already started the race and are approaching the halfway point. The student without a partner looks around anxiously. Finally, an older student who has finished grabs his ankles and they head out.

After the exercises and races, the children play a game or two. One of them is a game I played as a child in Japan called, "Pillow Grab." It's fun and provides a lot of exercise. The students split into two groups. Each group has few small pillows. The object is to capture pillows from the other team. Of course, there's no punching, kicking, or scratching allowed. Each team develops a plan of attack. They decide who will defend the pillows and who will go after the opponents' pillows. It requires a great amount of teamwork. Before long, they are all panting and sweating. They have shed their heavy workout uniform shirts and are wearing only their T-shirts.

They start to look at the clock on the wall. The end of class is drawing near, but they don't want their game to end. Finally, the instructor shouts, "Line up!" The students find their uniforms and put them on neatly before lining up. "*Arigato gozaimashita!*" (Thank you very much) says the instructor as he leaves the mat. The children thank each other, then run to the shoe rack. There, they grab their shoes and run to the lobby, where their parents are waiting for them. Every child is more alert and energetic than when the class began. A student runs back to the *dojo* to pick up his belt, which he left behind. "Bye, Sensei!" he shouts as he again runs out the door.

What I have described is a typical children's class. Of course, each class is unique, but all classes have the same general structure. If you have seen a children's martial arts class in which the students stand at attention, and make stiff movements in unison as the instructor shouts out orders, the scene described above may seem unstructured. That's part of the point of Aikido practice. I try to give the students as many opportunities as possible to communicate naturally with one another. I let them work things out together. They are always free to teach each other and to help each other. They don't have to pay strict attention to the instructor at all time, and they don't have to wait for an instructor to tell them when they can move and when they can't.

In Aikido classes — especially children's classes — instructors maintain a distance between themselves and their students. This gives the children the freedom to develop their own personalities and to establish their own goals. The fundamental role of an instructor at Nippon Kan is not so much to teach techniques, but to let the students learn things for themselves.

GIVING CHILDREN THE FREEDOM TO LEARN

When I say that Aikido students are encouraged to learn things for themselves, I don't mean that they don't need supervision or that they are left alone to do whatever they like. But whenever possible, instructors avoid intervening when students are interacting. Instead, they try to keep their distance and occasionally offer advice. Students learn to teach each other, to comfort each other, to discuss problems with each other, to yield to each other. If intervention is required, the instructor is always ready to take quick action.

Often, when we think of teaching children, we assume that it is best to give them specific instructions and to make sure that the instructions are followed precisely. But I think what is important is to let children discover things for themselves — in this case through the practice of a martial art. Too often, children learn things not by doing but by watching. It's not surprising that the kind of violence children see on television and in movies often finds a way into their lives. Children who are exposed to violence become less sensitive to violence.

As a martial arts teacher, I have long thought about what I can do to make children and parents understand that violence is never the proper solution to a problem. This book is one of the results. I want to help make parents understand that martial arts training can be much more than an exercise in baby sitting; that wearing pretty, colored belts is not a lofty goal. Over the years, I have tried to learn as much as possible about Americans and how Americans raise their children. And I have tried to make the practice of Aikido fit the times and the circumstances. The "way" of martial arts (*Budo*) is most meaningful when it can be applied to the real world, real living. If it is not useful in everyday life, it is no more than a relic.

I have used many words to explain to parents the effect that martial art training can have on their children. I am an Aikido instructor, so naturally much of what I have written is about how Aikido can affect children. Some readers may get the impression that I have nothing good to say about other martial arts and other *dojos*. I hope that this is not the case. My criticism is not aimed at any particular martial art. The problem is that martial arts in general have lost much of what they originally had to offer. Martial arts have become big business. Many instructors are more concerned about financial success than the well-being of their students.

If this book accomplishes nothing else, I hope that at the very least it will encourage parents to get more involved in their childrens' education. However, the bottom line is that parents must decide for themselves what is best for their children.

PART 2

CHILDREN'S
BASIC TECHNIQUES

INTRODUCTION

In the first chapter I discussed my philosophy of children's practice of Aikido. The focus of this chapter will be on specific Aikido techniques, introducing traditional etiquette, such as removing one's shoes and wearing proper clothing or uniforms, common to martial art schools. Aikido students, for example, must understand how to sit in *seiza* (kneeling) position and how to bow. Certain stretching, warm-up, and basic movement exercises make up the Aikido exercise section of this chapter. We will also use illustrations to introduce a number of beginning-level Aikido techniques.

Usually, manuals designed to teach martial art techniques stress rigid step-by-step movements. This book does not stress exact movement but focuses rather on general movement concepts. At Nippon Kan we believe that communication is just as important as physical training. The many different kinds of children that gather for Aikido classes have much to teach each other just by sharing. Because we believe that communication is vital to growth, Nippon Kan does not offer private lessons.

This book is not intended to be one that you can set on the living room floor, push back the furniture, and use to teach your child Aikido by following diagrams. It is a guide for concerned parents who want to further understand martial art training and the effect it might have on their children. I have written this book for them and for Aikido instructors who currently teach Aikido to children or are planning to do so. For these readers, the ABCs of Aikido movements are secondary to determining what in the discipline is healthy and positive for children. What makes a child feel comfortable?

Aikido should be practiced on a soft mat under the supervision of a qualified instructor. It needs to be practiced in a controlled and safe environment. It is not intended for the living room floor. Practicing Aikido offers stimulation to joints and muscles, from stretching, twisting, and spinning motions not found in sports like baseball, soccer, or swimming. Aikido is symmetrical in that you exercise both sides of your body equally. Aikido training can provide children, as well as adults, with an improved sense of balance.

If you plan to use this book as a text for a children's class, don't try to do everything at once. I recommend that you develop a long-term program using different combinations of exercise and techniques. Children become tired and bored easily. Use two sets of five repetitions on the left and right sides for each exercise. Plan to spend about ten to fifteen minutes for each technique, changing partners about every five minutes. This breaks up the routine and keeps the class interesting.

When you demonstrate the technique in front of the children, try not to be too fast and powerful. It is better to demonstrate slowly and calmly. Rigorous demonstration tends to create an atmosphere of competition that children respond to. Keeping your demonstrations slow and calm is also an important way to prevent accidents. Children watch carefully when you demonstrate an exercise or technique; you display a skill they wish to emulate. It is very important that you explain to them that your abilities are a result of an on-going process, that it took you a long time to become an instructor. If you do not explain this, you will not be an effective example. When I teach, I balance pride with a sense of responsibility. I never give wild, violent demonstrations for the children to marvel at. I do not seek exclamations of admiration from the class. Instead, I try to reach the children by going to their level and being a friend. Like an elementary school teacher, I maintain a position just a small distance ahead of the students. As their abilities improve, the distance between us stays the same. Instructors need not be on pedestals.

With each technique in this book I have included teaching pointers and advice to give to students during actual practice. Timing and delivery are very important. Present the children with questions or problems for them to solve. Encourage them to question on their own and figure out the answers. Each time a child comes up with a question on his own, repeat the question to the other children. Repeating the question and having the children answer aloud multiplies its effectiveness as a teaching tool. For example, if you as the instructor ask, "If someone without warning jumps out at you, what should you do?"

Answer: "First, you need to move to the safest place."

"Right. From a safe place you can see what is happening around you. Okay, lets keep this idea in mind and practice. This time your partner punches, what do you do?"

You have already given the answer to the question, but restructuring the question and asking it again serves to reinforce the lesson.

Use movements to ask and answer questions. After practicing for a time stop and compliment everyone's movement. "Very good, nice movement, but why are you stiff?" Demonstrate stiff, tight movements with a tight, exaggerated expression on your face. Then continue. "Just move the way you usually do. The next time you look in a mirror make a stiff pose and look at your face. That's not the way your face usually looks. Your usual face is the best face; it shows your nice self, your strong self. When a problem comes up it is best to greet it wearing your usual face, rather than something unnatural."

An important teaching technique is to ask questions, get the children to answer, and then practice the answer physically. Questions, answers, action. This teaching method works not only for the children's class, but adult classes as well. It is based on the idea that students need to find answers for themselves. I give hints or ask questions that prompt them to discover answers on their own. During this process I am there as a guide. Another element of my philosophy is that instructors need not teach "this is absolutely the way this is to be done." Getting students to think on their own is extremely important.

This chapter includes many tips for instructor-student conversations during class. It also includes "teaching points" for things to keep in mind when preparing for practice. All of the teaching points are general in nature; they can be applied to any technique. The names used for the exercises and techniques are those used at Nippon Kan. Names sometimes vary slightly from school to school. Those that simply cannot be translated into English will be left in the original Japanese (with brief descriptions). When we practice techniques, the person on the offensive is called the "approach person." We also call each other "partners." We use these terms for a reason. In children's class we try not to use the terms "offense," "defense," or "attack." We do this because to emphasize that Aikido is meant to unify and harmonize, not to polarize. However, because this book is a teaching guide, we will use the term "uke" or "offense side" to refer to the person that is attacking and "nage" as the person executing the technique.

In fifteen years Nippon Kan's children's Aikido class has never had a accident that required medical attention.

Healthy practice requires a safe environment, qualified instructors, and constant monitoring of the children. It is essential that the children be supervised properly to ensure that they are not attempting potentially dangerous techniques that are beyond their skills.

CLOTHES

WEARING PLAYCLOTHES

As I mentioned in Chapter 1, we do not require children to wear uniforms (*keiko-gi*) on the first day of class. Nor do we offer free *keiko-gis* as a package with boosted registration fees. In the beginning safe, comfortable playclothes or sweats are suitable. There are many reasons parents may have for not wanting to rush out and buy new uniforms right away. The most obvious one is the waste if the child does not continue. The primary goal should be to get the children on the mat to experience what Aikido is; what they happen to be wearing, as long as it is safe, is unimportant.

If you buy a uniform because it makes your child look cute or strong, remember that this is a reflection of your internal image of stars from the movies! Loose comfortable clothing is best. I do not recommend jeans or denim pants. All jewelry should be removed and pockets emptied. Basic hygiene and safety calls for fingernails and toenails to be trimmed and hands and feet to be clean. Long hair should be tied back in a ponytail or braid.

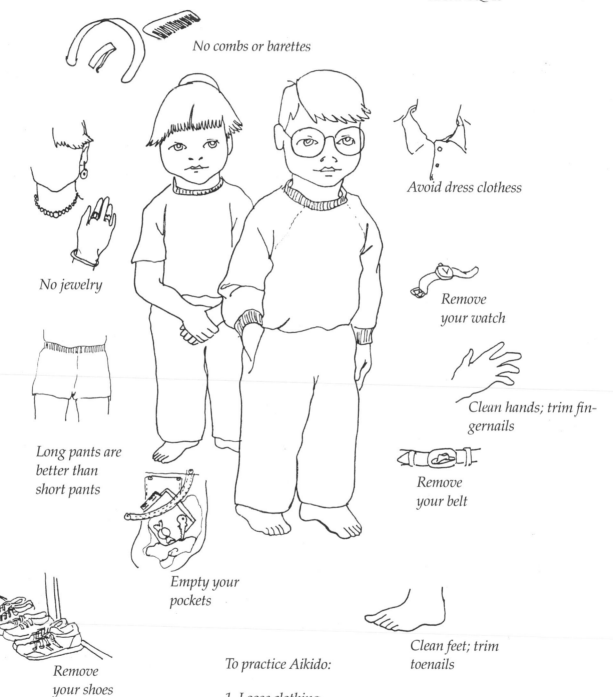

No combs or barettes

Avoid dress clothess

No jewelry

Remove
your watch

Clean hands; trim fin-
gernails

Long pants are
better than
short pants

Remove
your belt

Empty your
pockets

Clean feet; trim
toenails

Remove
your shoes

To practice Aikido:

1. Loose clothing.

2. Empty pockets.

3. Clean hands and feet.

WEARING A UNIFORM

Aikido does not have a special uniform designated solely for the practice of Aikido. Uniforms worn to practice Judo or Karate are called *keiko-gis*. "*Keiko*" means practice and the "*gi*" means to wear. In the United States uniforms are frequently called just "*gis*" — this is not the case in Japan. Either a Judo or Karate *keiko-gi* is appropriate to practice Aikido.

When purchasing a *keiko-gi*, check to see if the uniform is 100% cotton. If it is, open up the jacket and measure the sleeve against your child's arm. The edge of the cuff should reach to the middle of their hand. It is better that the uniform be a little big. Cotton will shrink two to three inches if washed in hot water. Karate *keiko-gis* can be made of many blends as well as 100% cotton, so check the label carefully. This formula for shrinkage applies only to 100% cotton *keiko-gis*. Karate *keiko-gis* are already white, but Judo *keiko-gis* are usually a light cream color. The uniforms of senior students turn very white from continual washing. Bleach can damage the fibers and reduce the life of the uniform.

There is a traditional way to put on a uniform. First take off your shirt and put on the uniform jacket. Then take off your street pants and put on the uniform pants. This pattern is based on a traditional martial arts concept that if you take off all your clothes, an emergency could literally catch with your pants down! Instructors should occasionally spot-check the dressing rooms to make sure the children are not leaving their street clothes strewn about carelessly. If the dressing rooms are a mess, direct the children to fold their clothes properly.

It is a good idea to label a child's uniform. Instead of writing directly on the uniform, write your child's name on a small piece of cloth and sew it onto the jacket. This way the uniform can be handed down to another child when it is outgrown.

The most challenging part of the Aikido uniform is the belt. There are always a few children in the class who spend most of their class time trying to keep their belts tied. Sometimes this is an excuse for not being able to do a technique or because they are tired, but mostly it is because the belt is tied incorrectly. Follow the directions accompanying the illustration to keep the belt on securely. After the belt has been tied, the tail ends should be about a foot long. If they are shorter, the belt will continually come untied. If they are much longer, they can get in the way during front rolls and practice.

In hot weather I have seen not only children, but adults and even instructors with their sleeves rolled up. I do not recommend this because your partner's fingers can get caught and twisted in the folds. This is especially true for those practicing breakrolls. Conversely, Aikido uses many wrist grabs, so it is also good not to have long sleeves covering your wrists. If sleeves are too long or too hot the simplest answer is to cut them off and hem them up.

How to wear your uniform

1. *Don't take off all of your street clothes at once. First remove your top and put on the jacket.*

2. *Put on the pants. Tie the draw string in the front with a bow.*

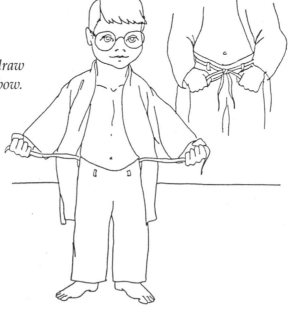

3. Tuck the right side of the jacket under the left. To tie the belt, first hold it in the middle in both hands in front of you. Hold the belt against your stomach and bring the ends around behind your back, crossing in the middle. Bring the ends to the front.

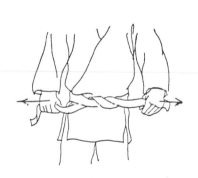

4. Tuck the right side under both ends as illustrated. Pull them to tighten.

5. Tie one more knot, starting by bending the right end up as illustrated. Pull both ends to tighten.

SEIZA
The Basic Sitting Position

To sit properly in *seiza* it is important to keep your back straight and your chin back (not jutting forward). To sit in *seiza* from a standing position, step back slightly with your left foot, then touch your left knee to the mat keeping your toes bent. Then place your right knee on the mat while keeping your weight on your toes arched forward. Then fold your toes down until you are sitting on the tops of your feet. Your big toes should overlap slightly; the left big toe under the right. I have occasionally seen people cross both feet underneath them. This throws the body out of balance and makes it impossible to sit with your back completely straight.

Your hands rest lightly palm down on the tops of your thighs, shoulders relaxed. Boys' knees should be about three fist widths apart. Girl's knees should be two fists apart. (This tradition stems from the constraints of traditional Japanese clothing and manners.) At Nippon Kan we observe this tradition as part of the etiquette of a traditional *dojo*.

SEIZA REI
Bowing from Seiza

To bow properly from *seiza*, place your left hand palm down on the mat in front of you, then the right hand, index fingers and thumbs touching slightly. Keeping your back straight, bow until your face is a few inches above your hands. Raise up and replace your hands on your thighs, right hand first, then the left. You should remain bowed for about three seconds. Bow in this manner with your head very low when entering or leaving the mat, bowing to the front of the *dojo*, and when bowing to the *sensei* (instructor).

When bowing to your partner during practice, lowering your head to about a 45° angle is sufficient. You want to be able to keep an eye on what your partner is doing.

These are the basic guidelines for bowing, but I do not encourage instructors to strictly enforce rules of bowing etiquette. As I mentioned in Chapter 1, good manners and proper etiquette should derive from respect rather than the adherence to strict rules.

Seiza

1. *Bend your left knee to mat, keeping your toes arched.*

2. *Bend your right knee and toes in the same way then release your toes so your feet lie flat on the mat, big toes overlapping slightly. Rest your hands palm-down on your thighs, fingers pointing slightly inward. (To stand up, reverse the previous motions.)*

1   2   3   4

Seiza rei (above)

3. *Place your left palm on the mat, then your right.*

4. *Keeping your back straight, bow forward. (To raise up, reverse the previous motions.)*

JŪNAN TAISO
Stretch Exercises

It is important to remember that children can be fragile. Stretches should never be done with force; they should be done at a pace that is comfortable for the children rather than the instructor. I never have partners push or pull each other when stretching. If a child pushes his or her partner too far they will stiffen. Accidents can occur if the child pushing is insensitive to his or her partner.

The instructor shouldn't bark "harder, harder, stretch further" — it just makes them sad and uncomfortable. If you notice a particularly stiff child, position yourself next to him and move stiffly yourself. Then gently challenge him to a stretching contest while offering lots of encouragement. The best policy is for everyone to stretch themselves. It is very difficult to injure yourself by pushing yourself past your own limit. For each exercise, use a count of five to each side. A few times is enough. Each child should join in and count along in a loud voice. To use your voice you need to exhale. Timing the voice count with the movement coordinates the breathing and the stretch. This is one of the major objectives of these exercises.

During stretch exercises use the time to talk to the children. For example: "How does everybody feel today? Are all the parts working? Good! Does it hurt a little bit? Me too, but let's try to stretch a little farther, okay? What would happen if we couldn't feel pain? What would happen if you broke your arm and you couldn't feel it? Pain is your body's alarm system. If we stretch and make it hurt just a little bit on purpose we can check our body's alarm system."

At the point when we sit and rotate our ankles I often explain: "How often do you check the bottom of your feet? On cold snowy days your feet snuggle in your boots. On hot summer days they run in the hot sand and play in the cold water. Your feet work very hard for you. They take you everywhere, anywhere you want to go. We need to take good care of them." These are just a couple of examples of conversation that you can make during stretch exercises. Again, it is best to phrase your points as questions to draw out reactions from the children.

Sometimes during knee bends there are children whose knees make a popping sound. This is a good opportunity to make a point. "Wow, what a racket! You know that if you don't get enough exercise your body can get mad and make noises at you!" I have found that the children today seem literally "weak in the knees." Focus on these exercises for those who seem stiff.

It is very important to do stretch exercises with hands open and extended. To explain the physiological reasons for this is not terribly important (or particularly easy). You can, however, demonstrate the reason physically. "Okay, everyone make tight fists and do this exercise. What did that feel like? Do it again and look at the person next to you. Now open your hands wide and try it again. Does that feel better? If it feels good it means it's good for you." Letting children experience the difference between how it feels to do an exercise with fists closed and then hands open will make the point better. To simply tell them to "open your hands, it is good for you" is not as effective. It is important to repeat often the importantance of taking care of your body.

One-leg stretch

1. *Extend your left leg out, back straight.*

2. *Open your fingers wide and stretch forward, trying to touch your forehead to your knee.*

3. *Exhale as you stretch forward, inhale as you raise up. Do this to count of five. Repeat on the right side to a count of five. Repeat the series a few times.*

Two-leg stretch

1. *Extend both legs out, back straight.*

2. *Open your fingers wide and stretch forward, trying to touch your forhead to your knees.*

3. *Exhale as you stretch forward, inhale as you raise up. Do this to a count of five. Repeat the series a few times.*

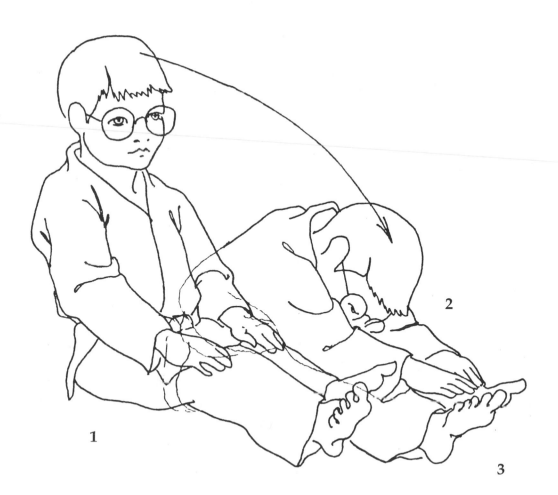

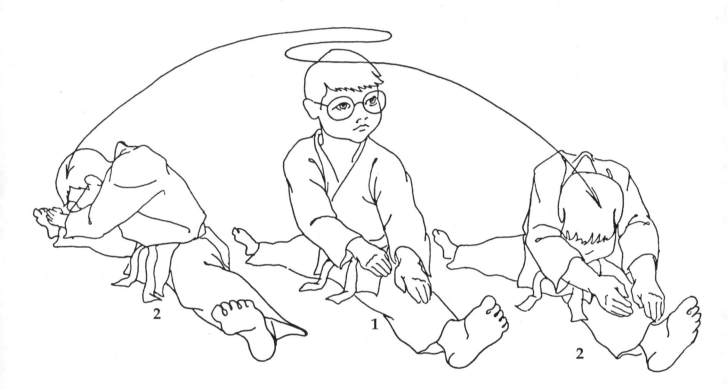

Open-leg side stretch

1. *Spread your legs as wide as you can.*

2. *Keeping your back straight, lean to the left side with your hands open wide. Do this to a count of five. Exhale as you stretch forward, inhale as you raise up. Repeat on the right side to a count of five. Repeat the series a few times.*

Open-leg center stretch

1. *Spread your legs as wide as you can.*

2. *Keeping your back straight and your hands open wide, reach your forehead to the mat. (Eventually, try to touch your stomach to the mat.) Do this to a count of five. Exhale as you stretch forward, inhale as you raise up. Repeat on the right side to a count of five. Repeat the series a few times.*

Foot and ankle stretch

1. *Hold you left foot in your lap and rotate each toe.*

2. *Next, rotate the ankle both ways.*

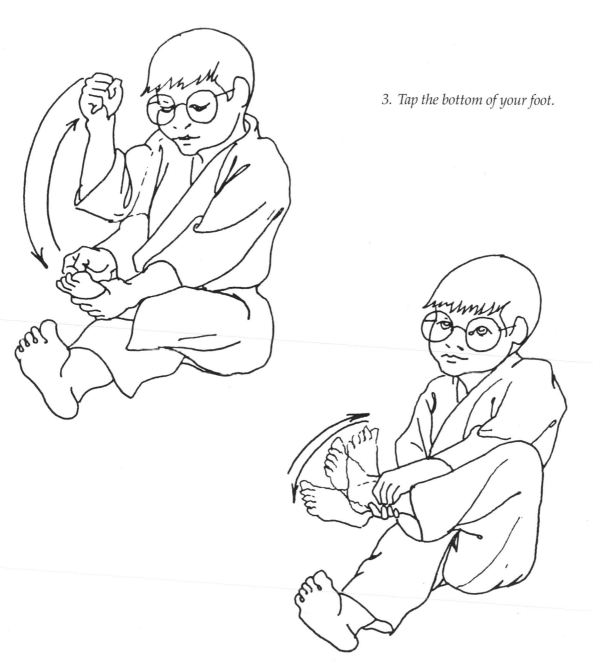

3. *Tap the bottom of your foot.*

4. *Shake your foot.*

Body Tap

1. *Extend your left arm out in front and tap the outside of your arm with the right fist. After several hits, switch and extend your right arm, striking with the left fist.*

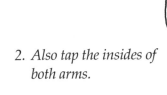

2. *Also tap the insides of both arms.*

3. *With your right fist, tap your left shoulder, chest and neck.*

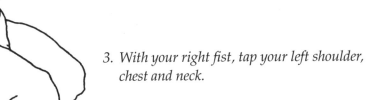

4. *Repeat on the right side.*

5. *Tap both thighs.*

6. *Repeat a few times*

Neck and shoulder stretch

1. *Sitting in seiza position, raise and rotate your shoulders backwards and forwards.*

2. Tilt your head forwards and backwards, and from side to side.

3. With your eyes open and your mouth closed, rotate your head and neck in wide circles. Repeat a few times.

4. Keeping your arms straight and your hands open wide, rotate your arms forwards and backwards. Repeat a few times.

Upper body, leg, knee, and ankle stretch

1. *Standing with your legs wide apart, first bend your right knee deeply, keeping your
   left leg straight. Keep your back straight and face ahead. Return to the center and then
   bend your left knee deeply. Stretch twice on each side; repeat a few times. Exhale as
   you stretch forward, inhale as you raise up.*

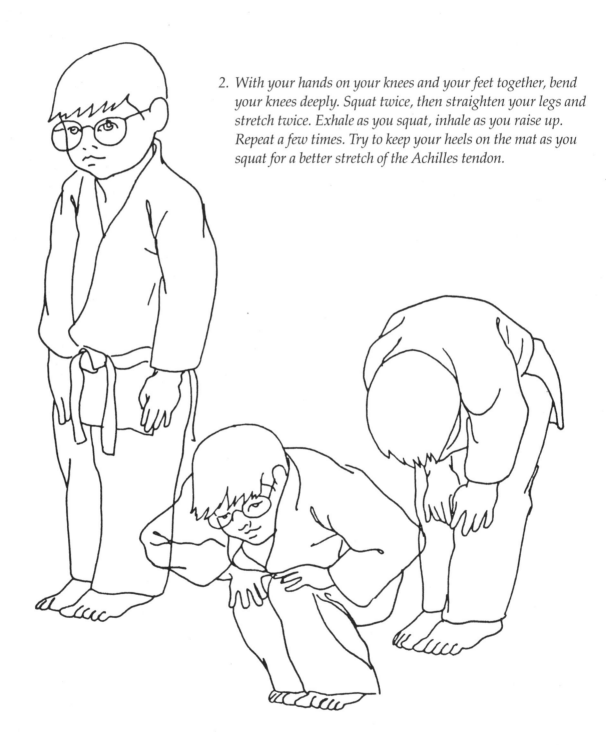

2. *With your hands on your knees and your feet together, bend your knees deeply. Squat twice, then straighten your legs and stretch twice. Exhale as you squat, inhale as you raise up. Repeat a few times. Try to keep your heels on the mat as you squat for a better stretch of the Achilles tendon.*

3. With your hands on your knees, swivel to make big circles parallel to the mat.

4. *Spread your feet and stretch both arms out to your sides, palms up. Stretch twice to the left side and twice to the right. Keep your back straight and face forward. Exhale as you bend, inhale as you raise up. Repeat a few times.*

5. *Spread your feet and stretch both arms over your head. Bend forward at the waist, twice to the front, then straighten and lean back. (To relieve pressure on your back, bend your knees when bending backwards.) Exhale as you bend forward, inhale as you bend backward. Repeat a few times.*

6. *Spread your feet and, with your hands outstretched, rotate at the waist in large circles counterclockwise. Repeat a few times.*

AIKI-TAISO
Aikido Exercises

These exercises shown in this section make up the basic movements used in the practice of Aikido techniques. When doing these exercises, make sure everyone joins in and counts along in a loud voice. Occasionally pick out a senior student and have them lead exercises while you give attention to individuals. When teaching beginners these exercises, you should explain and demonstrate how the movements are applied.

The movements in these exercises are simple, but if the instructor gives too much verbal detail the children will focus not on their own natural movements but on the instructor's voice. Therefore, it is better to explain the motions using demonstrations rather than speech. When you are teaching, usually you stand facing the children. When teaching new movements it is often helpful to turn around so you are facing the same direction they are.

These exercises are designed to work on body balance, and balanced movement — no one side of the body is favored over the other. Such movements include the *tenkan* (body spin movement), several wrist stimulations, and backrolls. These Aikido exercises usually follow the warm-up exercises, but they can also be a teaching tool during actual practice. If while teaching a technique the children seem confused on a movement, line them up and explain: "Okay, everyone is confused here. This movement is the same movement we do in our Aikido exercises, so let's do the exercise again."

It helps to pair the senior children with the beginners for one-on-one training. It is all right to overlook minor inaccuracies in what the senior student teaches, as long as it is not dangerous. What is important is the communication that takes place between the two. If there are small details to adjust, it is better to point them out when everyone is lined up doing the exercises together.

Ikkyo undo
First wrist stimulation

1. Hold your left hand out in front with your thumb
pointing down. Place your right hand over the knife
edge of the left with your right thumb pointed
toward your face.

2. With your shoulders relaxed,
pull your left hand toward
the center of your chest with
the right. Keep the fingers of
your left hand pointed away
from your body. Exhale as
you pull in.

3. Inhale and extend your arms
again. Repeat step 2 five times on
each hand (counting aloud).
Repeat a few times.

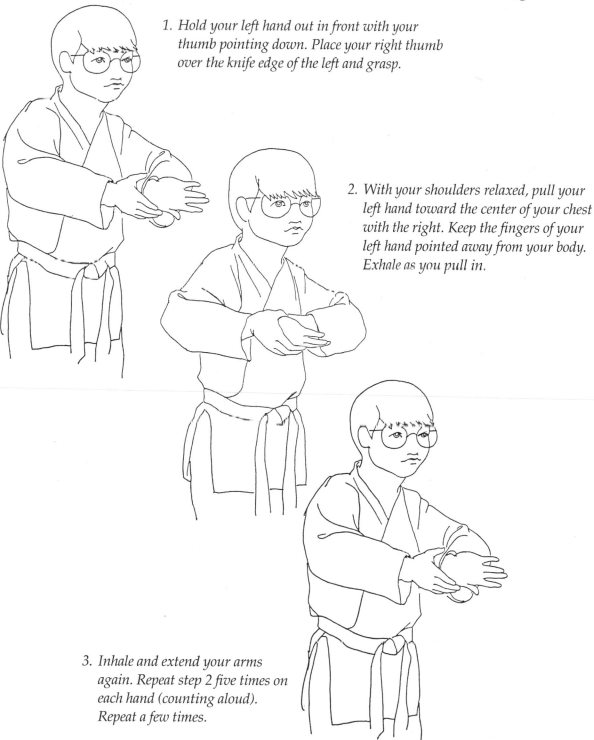

Nikyo undo
Second wrist stimulation

1. *Hold your left hand out in front with your thumb pointing down. Place your right thumb over the knife edge of the left and grasp.*

2. *With your shoulders relaxed, pull your left hand toward the center of your chest with the right. Keep the fingers of your left hand pointed away from your body. Exhale as you pull in.*

3. *Inhale and extend your arms again. Repeat step 2 five times on each hand (counting aloud). Repeat a few times.*

Sankyo undo
Third wrist stimulation 1

1. *Hold your left hand out in front with your thumb pointing down. With your right hand, reach over the knife edge of the left with your right thumb pointed toward your face. Bring the fingers of your right hands all the way around to the underside of your left hand.*

2. *Exhale as you twist your right thumb toward your face, bringing your left hand up toward your left side.*

3. *Inhale and extend your arms again. Repeat step 2 five times on each hand (counting aloud). Repeat a few times.*

Sankyo undo

Third wrist stimulation 2

1. Extend your left arm straight out in front, palm up. Grab the fingers with your right hand.

2. Exhale as you pull the fingers down and out from your body.

3. Inhale and extend your arms again. Repeat step 2 five times on each hand (counting aloud). Repeat a few times.

Yonkyo undo
Fourth wrist stimulation

1. *Hold your right hand out in front of you, fingers down, and palm toward you. Grab the inside of your right wrist, keeping the index finger of your left hand extended.*

2. *Exhale and push the ball of your left index finger into the right wrist.*

3. *Inhale and extend your arm up again. Repeat step 2 five times on each wrist (counting aloud). Repeat a few times.*

Kotegaeshi undo
Wrist twist stimulation

1. *Hold your left hand out in front of your face, palm toward you. Reach around behind with your right hand, with your fingers on the knife edge and your right thumb behind your left ring finger knuckle.*

2. *Exhale and twist down.*

3. *Inhale and bring your hand up again. Repeat step 2 five times on each wrist (counting aloud). Repeat a few times.*

Tekubi hado undo
Hand shake

1. *Keeping your shoulders relaxed, stand and shake your hands at your sides.*

2. *Raise your arms up over your head and shake your hands. Relax and let your hands drop back down to your sides.*

Fune kogi undo
Rowing

1. *Stand with your left foot forward.*

2. *Curl your hands down so that your wrists are forward and bring your elbows up.*

3. *Exhale and extend your arms forward to a count of one. Keep your back straight. Return the first position on a count of two. Repeat four or five times then repeat with the right foot forward.*

Ikkyo joge undo
Blocking

1. *Stand with your left foot forward.*

2. *Exhale as you extend your arms and raise both hands forward to eye level to a count of one. Keep your wrists lightly bent and your arms relaxed.*

3. *Return both arms to a relaxed position by your sides. Repeat four or five times then repeat with the right foot forward.*

1   2   3

Ikkyo zengo undo
Blocking front and back

1. *Stand with your left foot forward.*

2. *Exhale as you extend your arms and raise both hands forward to eye level to a count of one. Keep your wrists lightly bent and your arms relaxed.*

3. *Bring your hands down, pivot 180° on the balls of your feet and repeat step one to a count of two. Repeat a few times.*

3   1   2

Tenkan undo
Step pivot

1. *Stand with your left foot forward, hands out in front, palms up.*

2. *As you step forward with your right foot, turn your right hand over in a scooping motion.*

3. *Plant your right foot and step around 180° with the left.*

4. *Facing the opposition direction with your right foot forward, keep your back straight and step through with the left foot to repeat. Repeat a few times.*

1   2   3   4

Udefuri undo
Arm swing

1. *Standing with your shoulders relaxed, swing your arms from side to side, rotating your trunk from the waist.*

1

Iriminage undo

Step pivot with up and down arm movement

1. *Stand with your left foot forward, hands at your right side.*

2. *Inhale as you raise your arms and step forward with your right foot.*

3. *Swing your left foot back and lower your arms.*

4. *Facing the opposition direction with your right foot forward, keep your back
   straight and step through with the left foot to repeat. Repeat a few times.*

1   2   3   4

Tekubi kosa undo
Two-handed swing

1. *Standing with your feet comfortably apart, swing your hands together in front of your stomach. Repeat a few times to a count of five.*

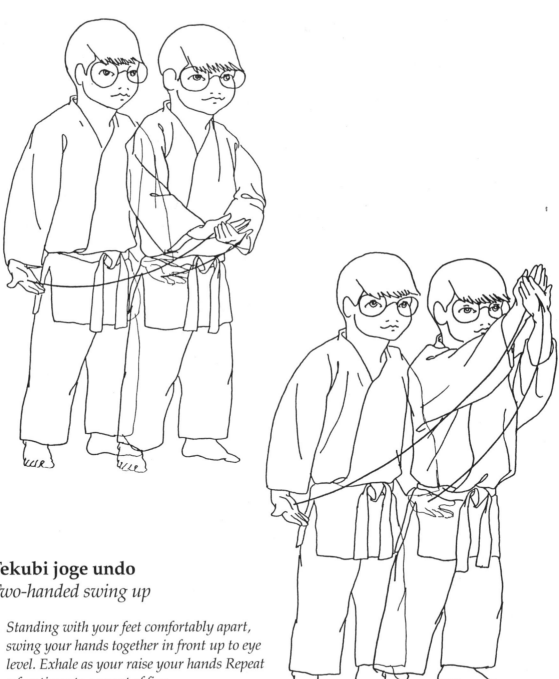

Tekubi joge undo
Two-handed swing up

1. *Standing with your feet comfortably apart, swing your hands together in front up to eye level. Exhale as your raise your hands Repeat a few times to a count of five.*

Sayu ido undo
Side swing

1. *Stand naturally with your feet apart. Inhale and step out with your left foot. Exhale as you bend your left knee and extend your arms left.*

2. *Return to your original position, step out with your right foot and swing your arms to right. Repeat a few times on both sides.*

2   1   2

Ushiro kakaedori undo
Grab-from-behind extension

1

2

3

1. *Stand naturally with your feet apart.*

2. *Step forward with your left foot to a count of one, extending your arms forward as shown in the illustration.*

3. *To a count of two, extend your left arm out and down as shown. Return to first position and repeat on right side. Repeat a few times.*

Ushiro tekubitori undo
Wrist-grab-from-behind extension

1. Stand naturally with your feet apart and curl your hands down.

2. Raise your arms up, inhale, and step forward with your left foot.

3. Exhale and bend forward at the waist. Return to first position and repeat on the other side.

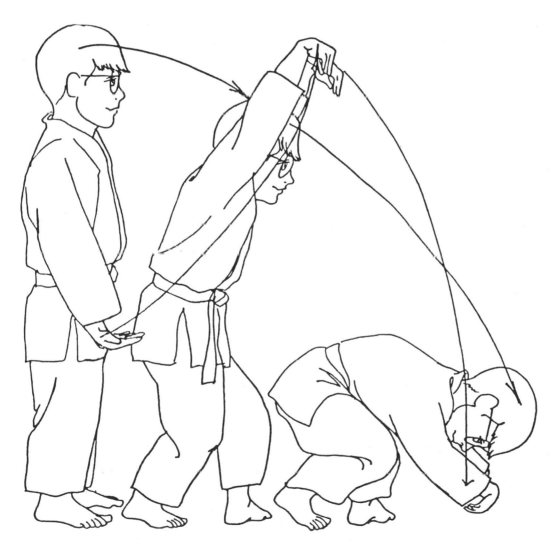

1   2   3

UKEMI
Falling and Rolling

When teaching children how to fall down or roll (the art of *ukemi*), there is one basic rule to follow. Do not use a step 1, step 2, step 3 approach. It is important to realize that too much step 1-2-3 can result in jerky movement. Instead, as the instructor, demonstrate by doing a small , smooth front roll. As explained in Chapter 1, children naturally love to tumble, to make round circular movements. What is dangerous is to demonstrate in front of beginning children or adults a big, high, flying, leaping front roll. Students will try to copy you and while they may have seen these rolls on television, they don't know how difficult they are or how painful it can be if you make a mistake.

If one of the senior students does a big roll, the beginning children, not knowing that it requires training, may jump in over their heads. If they get hurt or scare themselves, you have a larger problem that is not so easy to fix. Instructors need to be aware of the impression they make on children, and save the high-flying rolls for their own practice. When the children begin to roll or are practicing their *ukemi*, don't give them too much verbal advice. After they have started moving, they can get distracted by the sound of your voice. It can interrupt their flow of motion and cause accidents. Demonstrate a forward roll by starting in a squatting position low to the mat. Take the roll as if you were hugging a round ball. I have seen instructors try to explain to beginners how to roll from a standing position using "proper extension of the arm," etc. But, I think it is simpler to go back to the beginning. As I explained in Chapter 1, we started in the womb curled up in a ball, only as we grew did we learn to straighten up. It is natural for children to start learning to roll from a fetal-like position — they can work toward starting from a standing position.

When teaching rolls, you should begin with the basic backroll *(kihon ushiro ukemi)*, then move on to the other *ukemi* rolls. Children enjoy free rolls *(jiyu ukemi)*, which makes it easy to teach. Avoid collisions by preventing too many children from practicing at one time. The biggest risk of injury for children and adults alike is when people with little strength in their arms (and poor technique) attempt overly ambitious front rolls. A collapsed elbow means a landing on the shoulder. Instructors must keep a close watch for children who look like they might attempt flashy rolls beyond their ability.

Ushiro ukemi undo
Back roll

1. *Sit with your back straight and your legs crossed.*

2. *Keeping your hands out in front, roll back to a count of one. Tuck your chin down to protect your head.*

3. *Switch your legs and roll back up, exhaling as you come up. Repeat about ten times.*

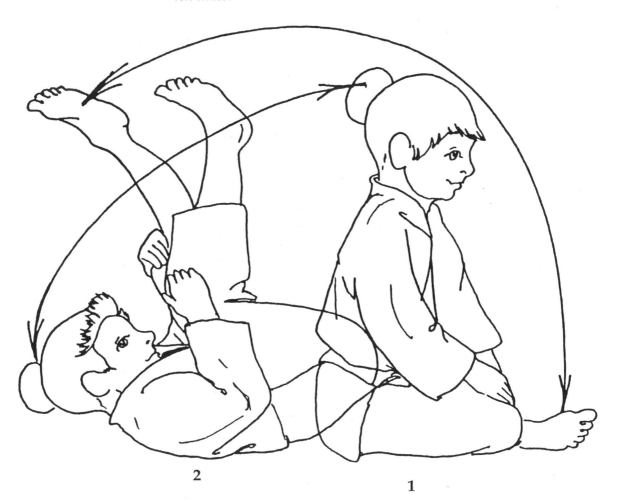

2   1

Tachi ushiro ukemi
Standing back roll

1. Standing naturally, tuck your left foot behind your right and gently fall back onto the mat. Round your back and tuck your head as for the backroll.

2. Rock forward keeping your left leg tucked, extend your arms, exhale, and push into a standing position.

3. Once standing, tuck your right foot behind your left and roll back and up as before. Switch feet again and repeat about 10 times.

Yoko ukemi undo
Side roll

1. *Lie flat on your back and look at the ceiling. Lift your left arm and leg up at the same time and roll to your left side; your palm slapping the mat, arm extended. (When practicing, it is better to not have your arm tucked close to your body during a fall.)*

2. *Return to the center, lift your right arm and leg and fall to the right side. Repeat about 10 times.*

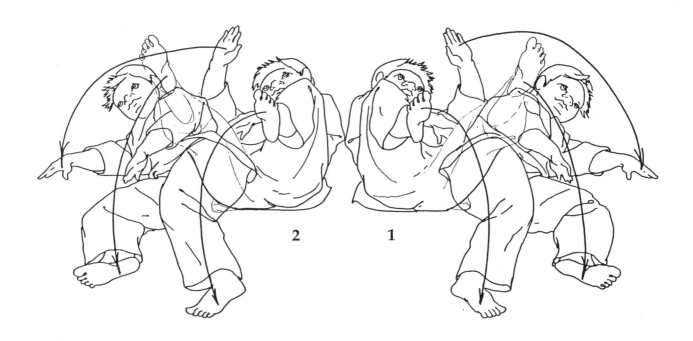

2   1

Tachi yoko ukemi
Standing side roll

1. *From a standing position, sweep your left foot forward and fall back on your left side, arm extended and palm down.*

2. *Return to a standing position, sweep your right foot forward and fall back on your right side. Repeat about ten times.*

2

1

Mae ukemi
Front rolls

1. *From a standing position, extend your left arm in a round arc, tuck your head, and roll forward in a small roll. Don't straighten or stiffen your arm, and don't jump forward onto your arm.*

2. *After you complete the roll, keep your left leg tucked and push yourself to a standing position.*

3. *Extend your right arm and roll on the right side. Repeat five to ten times. If you get dizzy sit, down at the edge of the mat.*

1

2

3

Ushiro ukemi
Back roll

1. *Start same as for a standing back roll. Tuck your left leg.*

2. *Instead of rolling back up, continue the backroll, tucking your head to one side, and continue the roll to a standing position.*

3. *Tuck your left leg and roll all the way back and over to a standing position. Repeat five to ten times. Look out for the person behind you.*

BASIC MOVEMENT

Aikido exercises are designed to be practiced individually. Basic Aikido movements focus on hand and arm movements, footwork, and body positioning. For the practice of Aikido techniques the children practice with partners: cooperation is by far the most important aspect of all Aikido techniques. Martial art instructors sometimes label partners. The person approaching to grab his partner becomes "the bad guy" and the person being grabbed becomes "the good guy." In this mind set the person being grabbed needs self-defense. In class we consciously avoid this approach. Instead, we try to impress on the children the idea of partnership. Each partner has his own job to do. When both partners do their jobs, matching their movements, they can successfully complete a technique. We avoid using words such as "opponent" and "attack," instead we use words like "partner's approach." We give equal attention to teaching both parts of the technique, not concentrating only on what the "defensive" position action should be.

When teaching the "approach" side of the technique the point is not on how to hit or punch someone with the most skill. We focus on showing how their action initiates a response and how they in turn flow with their partner's movements. At beginning levels, having students pretend they are acting can be a place to start. Even if they are "just acting" you are getting them to move together through a technique.

"If you hold your partner's wrist like this, and your partner steps back, you step too," etc. If you concentrate on teaching the defensive side only and don't teach both sides you can be faced with children who just stand there and drop their partner's hand in confusion. As in ballet lessons, partners move with partners to learn the movements. It is most important to teach how to move through the "approach" side of the technique to its completion; this gives the students the context for their movements.

Children sometimes have difficulty in smoothly leading their partners. When this happens, use more physical demonstrations. Slowly, rhythmically, with large movements, demonstrate both the "approach" side and "defensive" side to the technique. Children of today are visually oriented, absorbing a tremendous amount of their information from viewing media. Try not to give them too much detail verbally. A slow, visual demonstration is easier for them to follow and absorb. If you have a child who is having trouble coordinating his movements with his partner, try this advice. "Have you ever been fishing? If you pull the hook out of the water before the fish comes you will never catch a fish. Right? When your partner holds your wrist you have to move gently and carefully so they will stay with you. We are practicing this together. You can't go too fast and leave your partner behind. Make sure they can follow you to the end. Then you can finish the job together."

Gyaku hanmi katate tori-tenkan

One-handed grab with opposite feet forward outside body turn

1. *Extend hand being grabbed palm down. Curl your hand down, fingers toward you.*

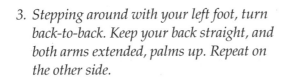

2. *Slide your right foot toward your partner's left foot.*

3. *Stepping around with your left foot, turn back-to-back. Keep your back straight, and both arms extended, palms up. Repeat on the other side.*

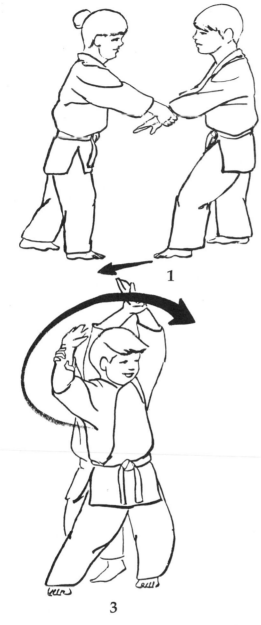

Ryotedori-mae tenkan
*Front-body turn out of a grab
of both hands*

1. *Open both your hands wide, palms down as your partner grabs.*

2. *Slide to one side with your outside foot.*

3. *Turn around to face the opposite direction. You should be standing next to your partner.*

4. *Extend your arms and gently give your partner a stretch. Repeat on the other side.*

Ryotedori-ushiro tenkan
Back turn out of a grab of both hands

1. *Open both your hands wide, palms down.*

2. *Keep your arms extended and slide back-to-back.*

3. *Turn around.*

4. *Extend your arms and gently give your partner a stretch. Repeat on the other side.*

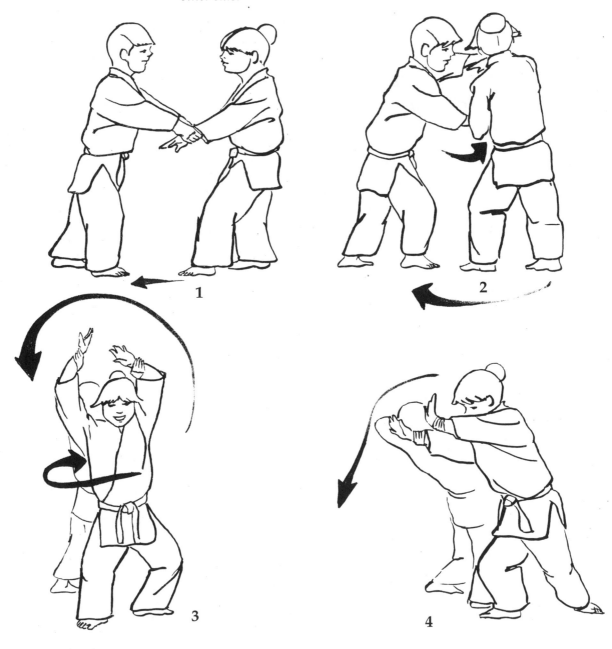

1

2

3

4

Gyaku hanmi katatetori-irimi

Entering movement out of one-handed grab with opposite feet forward

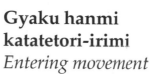

1

2

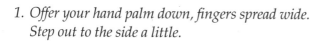

3

1. *Offer your hand palm down, fingers spread wide. Step out to the side a little.*

2. *Turn your hand as if your were turning a door knob.*

3. *Take one step in front of your partner and reach across them. Step behind your partner with your other foot and extend your arms forward, giving your partner a stretch. Repeat on the other side.*

Ryotedori-irimi
Entering movement out of a grab of both hands

1. *Offer both hands spread wide, palms down.*

2. *Step out to one side a little.*

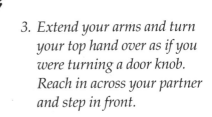

3. *Extend your arms and turn your top hand over as if you were turning a door knob. Reach in across your partner and step in front.*

4. *Step behind with your other foot.*

5. *Extend your arms forward and gently give your partner a stretch. Repeat on the other side.*

Gyaku hanmi katatetori-nagare tenkan

Leading turn out of a one-hand grab with opposite feet forward

1. Extend the hand your partner is going to grab.

2. Lead your partner into a big circle, turning toward your partner's backside.

3. Lead your partner into another circle, opening in front of you.

4. You should end up face-to-face on the opposite sides from where you began. Repeat on the other side.

Gyaku hanmi katatetori-nagare irimi

Entering out of a one-hand grab with opposite feet forward

1. *Extend the hand your partner is going to grab.*

2. *Lead your partner into a big circle, turning toward your partner's front.*

3. *You should end up face-to-face on the opposite sides from where you began.*

4. *Turn your hand as if you were turning a door knob and and reach across your partner. Take one step in front.*

1

2

3

5. *Step behind with your other foot and give your partner a gentle stretch. Repeat on the other side.*

4

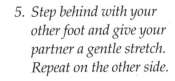

5

Ryotedori-nagare irimi
Leading entering movement out of a grab of both hands

1. *Offer both hands spread wide, palms down.*

2. *Lead your partner into a big circle, turning toward your partner's front.*

3. *You should end up face-to-face on the opposite sides from where you began.*

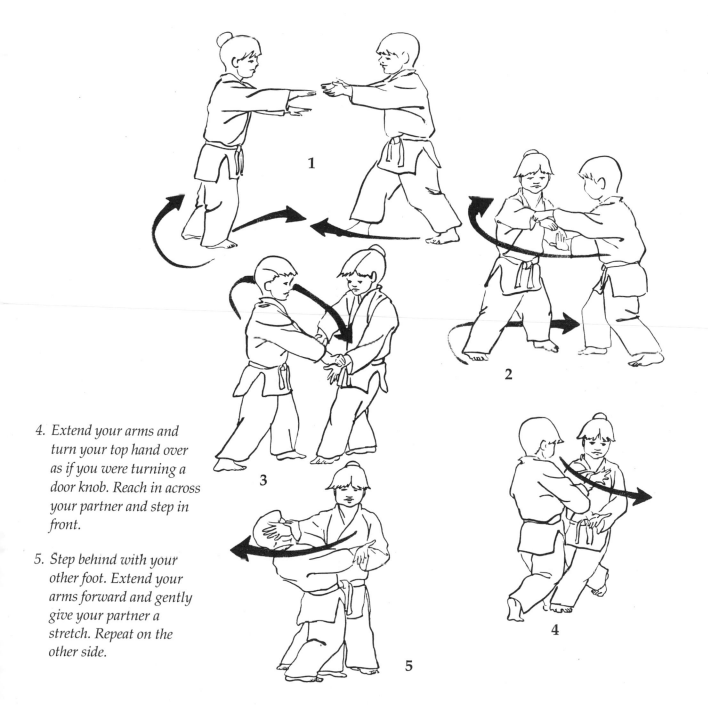

4. *Extend your arms and turn your top hand over as if you were turning a door knob. Reach in across your partner and step in front.*

5. *Step behind with your other foot. Extend your arms forward and gently give your partner a stretch. Repeat on the other side.*

A VARIETY OF APPROACHES

These four pages show examples of the many different ways partners can approach one another. The first step for partners is to find and understand the different positions created when one partner approaches another. To get things started I might say: "Where do you stand with your partner when you want to shake hands? How do you get ready to start to dance?"

As explained previously, Nippon Kan beginners classes substitute the word "approach" for "attack." Stressing true attack and defense positions can be a hindrance to learning Aikido. It is more important to get children to move in tandem like dancers or figure skaters.

This is more difficult to achieve if you have created the image that a child's partner is trying to ATTACK him. We try to encourage the child practicing the "defensive" side of the technique by saying, "Blending with your partner's motion is the most important thing, not how to fight, or how to beat up your partner. When we practice both sides are even: no winners, no losers, no good guys, no bad guys." It is very important to this get across to the children from the beginning.

Ai hanmi-katatetori
Same hand grab, palm down

Ai hanmi-katatetori
Same hand grab, palm up

Gyaku hanmi-katatetori
Opposite hand grab

Ryotedori
Both hands grab

Katatetori-ryotemochi
Two hands grab one

Kubishime
Front choke

Kata munetori
One hand front lapel grab

Ryo munetori
Two-handed lapel grab

Katatetori-chokugeri
Opposite hand grab and straight kick

Katamunetori-shomenuchi
One-handed lapel grab and frontal strike

Katatetori-shomentsuki
Opposite hand grab and punch

Ushiro-ryotekubitori
*Grab of both hands
from behind*

Ushiro-ryohigitori
*Grab of both elbows
from behind*

Ushiro-ryokatatori
*Both shoulders grabbed
from behind*

Ushiro-eritori
*Collar grabbed
from behind*

Ushiro-kakaetori
Body hold from behind

Ushiro-katatetori kubishime
One hand grab from behind and choke

Yokomen uchi
Side strike

Shomen uchi
Straight, frontal strike

Mune tsuki
Straight punch

Choku geri
Straight kick

Ganmen tsuki
Upper punch

Mawashi geri
Round kick

Yoko geri
Side kick

SHOMEN UCHI
Straight Frontal Strike

Shomen uchi — kote gaeshi
Frontal strike, outward wrist twist

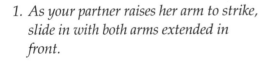

1. As your partner raises her arm to strike, slide in with both arms extended in front.

2. Stepping around with your right foot, turn back to back.

Classtime conversation

"Your partner is trying to hit you. Right? Why? What could have happened that he is trying to hit you? It's all right, just move like you did in the exercises, the same movement. If you try to block that hand it hurts doesn't it? Anyway, if you try to block and can't, then what? Once your partner starts to move around you, you move too. Try to make one smooth motion together."

Teaching points

Beginners sometimes focus all of their attention on the approaching hand, trying to reach out and grab it. If you see this, try demonstrating correct body movement by going through the technique with your hands behind your back. This emphasizes movement over clutching at the striking hand. Teach the "approach side" partner how to move through his part of the technique all the way to the finish without resistance.

3. Continue to lead your partner in a circle now parallel to the mat.

4. Step away from your partner with your left foot and gently twist your partner's wrist.

6. Your partner drops back into a back roll.

5. Your partner tucks the same leg as the hand that's being twisted.

Shomen uchi — iriminage
Frontal strike, body throw

1. *Slide in toward your partner as your partner approaches.*

2. *Extend both arms forward and pivot on your right foot. (Step all the way behind your partner.)*

Classtime Conversation

"If you just stand there you will get hit! Move out! Where's the safest place to go? Yes, you have a problem in front of you. Someone is trying to hit you, but you don't know what may be happening behind you. Now do you know what to do? Right, turn and face the same direction your partner is facing. You can do this by doing the iriminage exercise. Let's practice just the exercise. See, by turning like this you can take care of your partner and see what is behind you."

Teaching Points

If the child approaching is too rough, teach the child who is in the defensive position the movement he is supposed to do. Then blindfold him loosely. This might sound strange, but children basically are kind and innocent at heart. A child who was being too rough will hesitate to be rough if his partner can't see. He should respond with a gentler, more cooperative approach. "Your partner can't see, help him or her.'

3. Reach for your partner's neck and hold your partner's head by your shoulder as your step back your right foot. Bring your partner with you as you step back.

4. Bend your partner over. Naturally, your partner will want to stand up.

5. As your partner stands up, take one more step forward and extend your arm. Your partner tucks his inside leg.

6. Your partner falls into a back roll.

Shomen uchi — ikkyo (irimi)
Frontal strike, first arm hold (front)

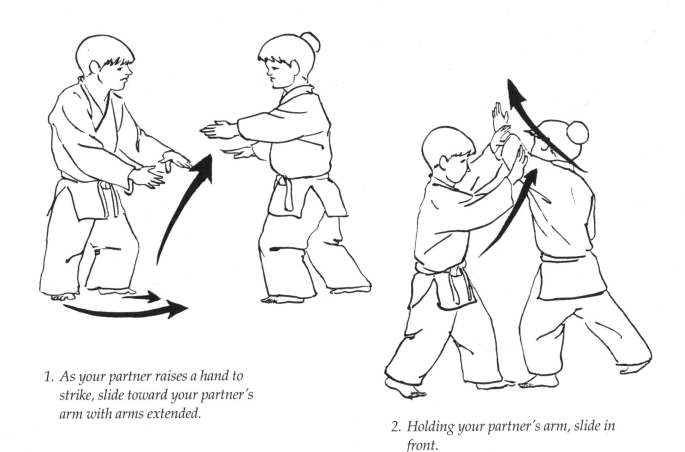

1. *As your partner raises a hand to strike, slide toward your partner's arm with arms extended.*

2. *Holding your partner's arm, slide in front.*

Classtime Conversation

"If your partner tries to hit you, you could kick back, but would that be the right thing to do? If you do, it is no different than being the school bully. But, if you don't do anything, you'll get hit. You have to do something. There is something you can do to protect yourself without hurting your partner. You can use this kind of technique."

Teaching Points

Instructors are usually more familiar with teaching the techniques used by the child in the defense position. More difficult is to teach the movement of the "approach side" partner. Occasionally demonstrate the approaching movement to its completion and lead the class in "approach side" practice. If you encounter children whose shoulders and arms are stiff during this practice, it is usually because they are apprehensive. Work individually with these children slowly and gently to remove their tension. "See, if you relax it is much easier and smooth, and you won't get hurt as easily."

3. Rotate your partner's arm
forward.

4. Take one more step
forward.

5. Bend your partner's wrist. This is the
first stimulation. When your partner
has had enough, your partner should
tap the mat.

GYAKU HANMI KATATETORI

Opposite Foot Forward, One-hand Grab

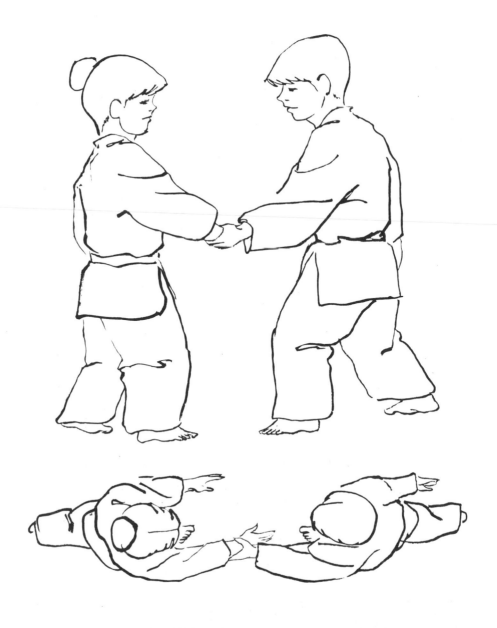

Gyaku hanmi katatetori — kotegaeshi
Wrist twist from opposite-hand grab with opposite feet forward

1. Step out to the side.

2. As in the two-hand swing exercise, raise both yours and your partner's arm up.

Classtime Conversation

"If someone you don't know is almost about to grab your hand, what do you do? If you are walking down the sidewalk and a bicycle is just about to run into you, what do you do? What is the best thing for you to do right now during practice? First you need to move your body to the safest area. We don't know yet why this person wants to grab your hand so we can't just start kicking and hitting back. Right? The best thing to do is to move a little bit out of the way and make sure what is happening. Then, by blending with your partner's movements as smoothly as possible, you can find a new direction, another way to go.

Teaching Points

If a problem occurs during practice, stay clam and relaxed and find out what the problem is. It is important that you, as the instructor, move calmly, observe the situation quietly and take care of the problem. In our practice it is precisely this ability to remain calm we are trying to teach. So it is important that you set an example for the children to emulate. Give a demonstration showing how movement and breathing work together. Using exaggerated movements, have a partner grab your hand with the opposite hand, step to the side and raise your hands up (as shown) and inhale. Hold your partner's wrist, turn and exhale. Open with a step to the side and inhale, then twist your partner's wrist and exhale.

3

4

3. Turn back-to-back, grabbing over the top of your partner's wrist.

4. Keep your arm extended and lead your partner around in a circle.

5. Gently twist your partner's wrist.

6. Your partner tucks the same foot as the hand being twisted.

7. Your partner drops into a back roll.

5

7

6

Gyaku hanmi katatetori — shihonage (irimi)
Entering four-direction throw from opposite-hand grab with opposite feet forward (front)

1. *Offer your hand to your partner palm down. Just as your partner grabs, step out to the side.*

2. *Using your free hand, grab your partner's hand and slide in front of your partner.*

Classtime Conversation

"See, it's just like dance. Hold your partner's hand gently, cross under in front. That's it. You have danced before, right? If you are stiff and rough, no one wants to dance with you. If you can't cross under in front, how about going around to your partner's back. If you can't go to the front, there is always the back. If you can't go to the back, there is always the front. There are many chances open to you."

Teaching Points

Learning to distinguish doing a technique to the front side (omote) or the backside (tenkan) can be confusing. Children worried about making mistakes can think and think until finally they can't move. If this happens, hold their index finger lightly as if you were doing a jitterbug or a folkdance to move them through the movement. This should soften them up. Then say, "OK, next it's your turn." Let them hold your finger and lead you softly through the movements. Change sides again and suggest they do a backroll after the movement is complete. This is a natural progression toward doing the entire technique. As the instructor, giving too much detailed instruction can cause more confusion than help. To avoid having children "freeze on the spot", keep your directions geared to the general body movement. If you ask a child to do a tenkan technique and they do the technique omote instead, don't correct them. Instead present a question: " There are two ways to do this technique movement — what is the difference between the two?"

3. *Slide all the way
under your partner's
arm then pivot.*

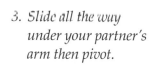

4. *Your partner tucks the same foot
as the arm being held.*

5. *Your partner drops into a back roll. As your
partner falls, let go of your partner's arm.*

Gyaku hanmi katatetori — shihonage (tenkan)

Turning four-direction throw from opposite-hand grab with opposite feet forward (behind)

1. Offer your partner your hand and lead your partner's movement.

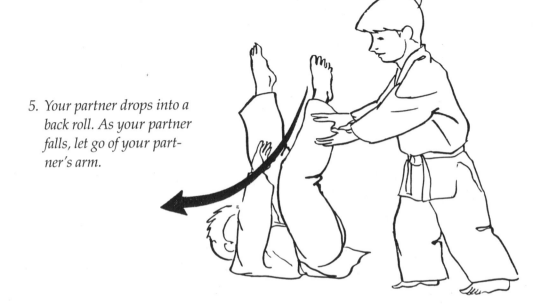

5. Your partner drops into a back roll. As your partner falls, let go of your partner's arm.

2. *Pivot smoothly with
your partner following.*

3. *Turn completely under
your partner's arm.*

4. *Your partner tucks the same
foot as the arm being held.*

Gyaku hanmi katatetori — iriminage
Body throw from opposite-hand grab with opposite feet forward

2. *Slide in with your other foot.*

1. *As your partner grabs, lead your partner's hand up and step off to the side.*

Classtime Conversation:

"When your partner comes to grab your hand, open your hand, step out, raise your hands high and inhale. Turn the same direction with your partner and exhale. As your partner starts to stand up, inhale, and take one more step behind your partner and exhale, down they go. You've been on a roller coaster, haven't you? It's the same feeling. Pretend you are the roller coaster heading up that first hill before going down fast on the other side. Repeat again. There comes your partner who grabs your hand and you raise your hands high. Then, like the roller coaster, plunge down the other side and into the first turn. Turn with your partner down and up again and down."

Teaching Points:

The roller coaster is not an example for children's class only. The changing speeds and direction of motion of the roller coaster takes is a good example for this technique for adult class as well. Training the mind to blend with the changing speed and up and down rhythm is as important as learning the footwork in the technique.

3. Step behind your partner, holding your partner's neck.

4. Step back and pivot in one motion.

6. Your partner drops into a backroll.

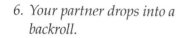

5. As your partner begins to stand up, take one more step forward. Your partner tucks the inside leg behind him.

Gyaku hanmi katatetori — kaitennage
Rolling throw from opposite-hand grab with opposite feet forward

2. *Step through under your partner's arm and turn to the outside.*

1. *As your partner grabs your hand, step to the side and raise up your partner's arm.*

Classtime Conversation:

"Yes, we are practicing how to do this technique, but at the same time we are practicing our front rolls. Just in case you slip sometime and start to fall down, you need to learn how to protect yourselves. This is what we are practicing, how to protect ourselves by learning how to front roll. It's your partner's turn to practice their front rolls, so you need to help him by being careful and gentle, so that he can do his front rolls easily."

Teaching Points:

Sometimes while a child is attempting the technique, the "approach side" partner lets go. One reason for this is that they don't know that they are suppose to hang on until they are ready to do the front roll. Another reason is the stigma that to have someone throw them means that they are the loser. It is important to tell them that this is front roll practice. Especially for children, front rolls are a big challenge. After completing a well-done front roll there is always a look of happiness and achievement. The children need to understand that they are not being thrown, but that they are executing a front roll to protect themselves.

3. While turning, make a big circle
forward with your hand, eventually
reaching behind you.

4. Grab your partner's wrist, and put your other hand
on your partner's neck, pressing down firmly.

6. If your partner does
not resist, your part-
ner will naturally fall
into a forward roll.

5. Taking one more step, gently project your
partner forward.

AI HANMI KATATETORI

Same Foot Forward Same Side One -hand Grab

Ai hanmi katatetori — kotegaeshi
Wrist twist from one hand grab with the same foot forward

2. *Grab over with your other hand.*

1. *Offer your hand to your partner extended with your palm up.*

Classtime Conversation

"What do you do when you want to shake hands? You open up your hand, right? That is the way you make new friends. If you are always holding up your fists you can't make friends. Your partners are very important; they help you practice and learn. When your partner holds your wrist, open your hand wide and lead your partner where you want him to go. This is the kind of feeling you want to have while you are going through the movement. Your partner helps you learn the techniques. When it is his turn, you have to be a good partner too, so that he can learn the techniques."

Teaching Points

If children practice a single technique over and over again with the same partner their movements can get sloppy and smaller. At Nippon Kan, we have the students do the movement on their own, without partners, following the instructor through the motions and making them large and exaggerated until they become "life size" again. It takes more time to complete a technique if you use big, extended movements than it does if you hurry through with small, tight movements. Sometimes children believe that to do a technique correctly, they have to do it as quickly as possible. Usually this results in techniques that are rough and too fast. To get them to slow down, try practicing to a waltz or slow New Age music. For the children to watch the instructor demonstrate to music can be helpful. At Nippon Kan, we have used music in both children's and adult classes.

3. Turn back to back.

4. Twist your partner's wrist.

5. Your partner tucks the same foot as the hand being twisted.

6. Your partner drops into a back roll.

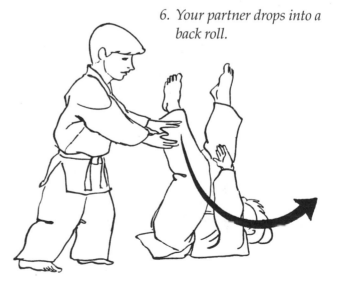

Ai hanmi katatetori — shihonage (irimi)
*Entering four-way throw from one hand grab
with the same foot forward (front)*

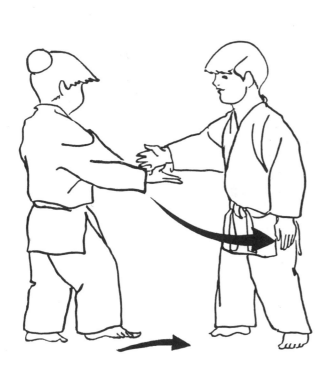

2. *As your partner grabs your hand, turn your
hand over to the palm down position, rotating
your partner's arm at the same time.*

1. *Offer your hand to your partner
extended with your palm up.*

Classtime Conversation

*"You are are not trying to make your partner move around you. You move first and your partner will follow
you. It doesn't matter which way you go, across the front or to the back, if you move you will find the right way.
The worst thing you can do is just stand there trying to decide, and not move at all. If you lay on the couch and
can't decide whether to do your homework or go out and play, you don't benefit from either. Make a move."*

Teaching Points

*Children usually get confused with techniques that go both to the front (irimi) and to the back (tenkan). At
Nippon Kan, we address this problem by playing "rewind." After making partners, we start the technique
once to the front and then "rewind" back to the starting position and then go to the back and "rewind" back to
the start again. The instructor can randomly call out "tenkan" or "irimi" to make an exercise out of the game.
This reinforces the footwork used to go to both sides.*

3. Step through all the way in front of
   your partner and turn.

4. Your partner tucks the same foot as
   the arm being held.

5. Your partner drops into a back roll.
   As your partner falls, let go of your
   partner's arm.

Ai hanmi katatetori — shihonage (tenkan)
Turning four-way throw from one hand grab with the same foot forward (behind)

2. *Sliding to the front, turn your hand over palm down, rotating your partner's arm at the same time.*

1. *Offer your hand to your partner extended with your palm up.*

Classtime Conversation
"If you want to do this technique and move toward the front of your partner and your partner resists you, what do you do? Don't worry; don't try to push back. Just change direction and turn to the back side instead."

Teaching Points
When doing tenkan techniques it is important to keep a careful eye on your partner, as illustrated in illustration 3. When executing the turn, make sure that the children extend their partners' arms up so that there is room to turn below their arms. If the arm is extended too far out and the technique is performed quickly, an arm injury can occur. On the other hand, if the extended arm is too high, the technique can turn into a dance step — with both partners turning. To avoid this, explain that everyone is being taught to lift their partner's arms to avoid injury.

3. Step behind your partner with your right foot.

4. Turn all the way under your partner's arm.

6. Your partner drops into a back roll. As your partner falls, let go of your partner's arm.

5. Your partner tucks the same foot as the arm being held.

Ai hanmi katatetori — iriminage
Body throw from one hand grab with the same foot forward

2. *Step behind your partner with the other foot.*

1. *Offer your hand to your partner palm up. Slide forward with the same foot.*

Classtime Conversation

"If you just stand in the same place and try to get your partner to move, it doesn't work very well, right? If you tried to ride a bike without pedaling you would fall over, right? The bicycle doesn't ride you, you ride the bicycle. This is the same thing, don't just wait for you partner to grab your wrist. You move first and bring your partner around with you."

Teaching Points

To practice the tenkan foot work, we do the "helicopter" exercise. The children lift both of their arms out-stretched and do the tenkan movement as if they were helicopters. Then we make partners and try to do the same balanced body spin exercise. This tenkan exercise is good for children whose movements are either stiff or small. It is difficult to do this exercise stiffly without losing your balance. With continued practice, stiffness disappears and balance improves.

4. *Holding your partner's neck, pivot,
bring them with you as you turn.*

3. *Reach for your partner's
neck.*

5. *Your partner will want to
stand up.*

6. *As your partner stands up, take one more step forward. Your partner tucks your partner's inside foot.*

7. *Your partner drops into a back roll.*

Ai hanmi katatetori — ikkyo
First arm hold from one hand grab with the same foot forward

2. *Slide in, raising your partner's arm in a wide circle to the outside.*

1. *Offer your hand to your partner palm down.*

Classtime Conversation

"The most important thing is to open you hand wide even before your partner grabs your wrist. Then make a big circle with your arm and touch your partner's elbow. As you push your partner's elbow forward pretend you are wiping the sweat from his face with his sleeve. You don't have to be rough, your partner can follow you easily. It is better to make a smooth wide circle so your partner can keep a hold of your wrist. Check your body stance. Is your back straight? Are you crouched over like a cat ready to pounce? When you go to school you don't walk like a cat, right? Make sure you are standing up straight."

Teaching Points

At Nippon Kan we spend a lot of time trying to keep upright posture during movement. Sometimes children can get a bit theatrical, active, silly, or flashy. This can lead to unnatural stances while they practice. To correct this, show them what their posing looks like by copying them, only exaggerate. Then explain, "At school or home you don't move like that; the best way to hold your body is to be natural, with your back straight."

3. Holding your partner's elbow,
   continue to slide closer.

4. Keeping your part-
   ner's arm bent, crank
   your partner's elbow
   forward.

5. Take one for step forward.

6. Bend your partner's wrist. This is the first stimulation. When your partner has had enough, he
   should tap the mat with his free hand.

RYOTEDORI
Two-hand Grab

Ryotedori — tenchinage
Sky and ground throw out of a grab of both hands

1. *Extend both hands toward your partner as your partner grabs.*

3. *As you slide to the outside, the left hand extends down toward the ground and the other extends up toward the sky in front of your partner's face.*

2. *Slide forward to the outside of your partner's front foot.*

4. *Take one more step forward. Your partner tucks his inside foot.*

5. *Your partner drops into a back roll.*

Classtime Conversation

"Your partner has grabbed both your wrists, right? But to do that your partner has used up both his hands. You haven't used your hands yet because you didn't grab. One thing you don't want to happen is to run into your partner head on. So as you are coming together, you move to the side a little and then back on the path you started. If you move like that when someone holds your wrists like this, they will fall down naturally."

Teaching Points

Teach the disadvantages of trying to match power with power in a head on struggle. Show the advantages of stepping out of the way just slightly and then getting back on track. Relate this concept to problems that come up in children's daily lives. "If you are having a hard time with somebody, instead of getting mad and pushing back, step to the side and then keep going your own way (figuratively as well as literally)."

Ryotedori — shihonage (irimi)
Four-direction throw out of a grab of both hands (front)

2. *Grab one or the other of your partner's hands.*

1. *Extend both hands toward your partner palms down.*

Classtime Conversation

"You know how to do shihonage already when your parnter holds one hand, right? This time, your partner holds both of your hands. Don't worry, this is not a problem, in fact it's better for you. This way you can choose either hand and make a technique."

Teaching Points

Children can be more intimidated by having both of their hands grabbed. Explain the positive side to this situation; that the partner has no more hands, he is using them both. This is training in positive thinking. Before you teach the actual technique, first start by letting the children find out for themselves which directions they can go starting out with one partner holding both of the other's hands. "When your partner holds both your hands, go ahead and move, find your way around." They will naturally find the technique by themselves. When they do, give them positive reinforcement. If you begin this technique by demonstrating and they go the wrong way, it can make them feel bad and slow down the learning process. This way they discover it for themselves.

3. Slide across the front of your partner.

4. Extend your partner's arm in front of you.

5. With your outside foot, slide all the way under your partner's arm and pivot.

7. Your partner drops into a back roll. As your partner falls, let go of your partner's arm.

6. Your partner tucks the same foot as the arm being held.

Ryotedori — shihonage (tenkan)
*Turning four-direction throw out of a grab
of both hands (behind)*

2. *Grab either of your partner's hands.*

1. *Offer both hands toward your
partner palms down as your partner grabs.*

7. *Your partner drops into a back roll. As
your partner falls, let go of your partner's arm.*

3. *Slide across the front of your partner.*

4. *Step behind your partner with your right foot.*

6. *Your partner tucks the same foot as the arm being held.*

5. *Turn all the way under your partner's arm.*

MUNE TSUKI
Punch

Mune tsuki — kotegaeshi
Wrist twist from a body punch

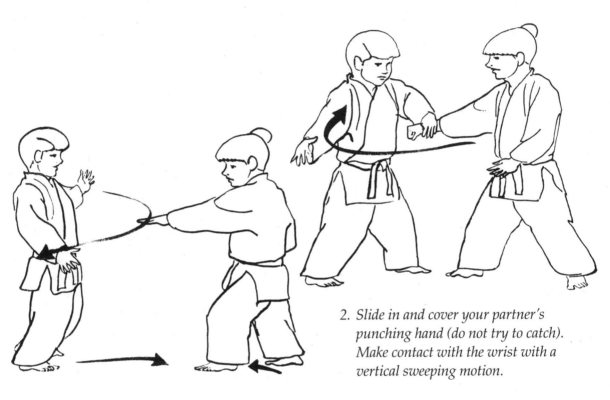

1. Give your partner a target.

2. Slide in and cover your partner's punching hand (do not try to catch). Make contact with the wrist with a vertical sweeping motion.

Classtime Conversation

"When you've been at school or out at play,has anyone ever come up and punched you? If this happened what did you do? Maybe there was a reason. If someone punches you, you don't need to try to block the punch and punch or kick back. The better thing to do is to just move, move to the safest place you can go, and at the same time check what is going on behind you. For this we need to practice doing a tenkan. Let's do the tenkan exercise now."

Teaching Points

Children pick up images from television and movies of flashy, violent heroes. Children that have practiced any of the striking martial arts are used to responding stiffly and punching back hard. Try to discourage this type of response. To children like this try saying, "Anyway, when, where, and against whom are you going to use a technique like that, and for what reason? It's a lot better to just move to a safe place and control the situation without hurting your partner." This is the kind of direction to give the children as they practice.

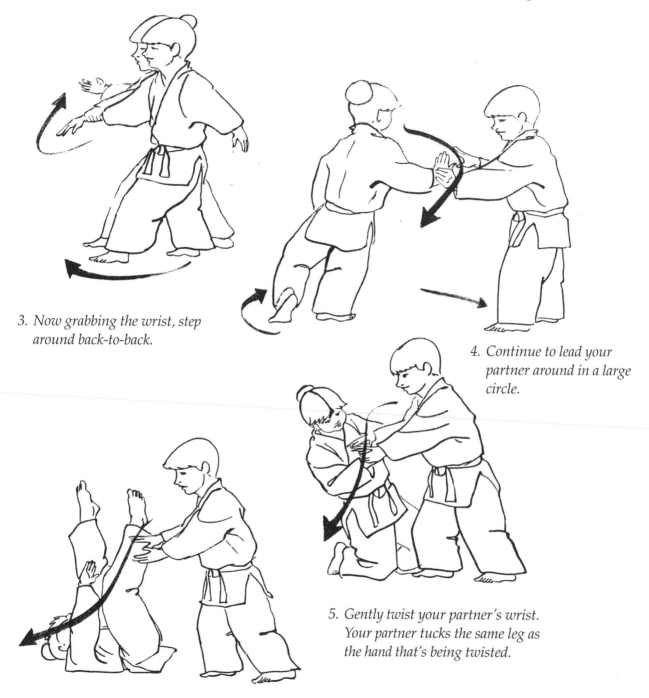

3. Now grabbing the wrist, step around back-to-back.

4. Continue to lead your partner around in a large circle.

5. Gently twist your partner's wrist. Your partner tucks the same leg as the hand that's being twisted.

6. Your partner drops into a back roll.

USHIRO RYOTEKUBITORI

*Both Hands Grabbed
from Behind*

Ushiro ryotekubitori — kotegaeshi
Wrist twist from both hands grabbed from behind

1. *As your partner moves toward you, offer your palm up and slide forward with the same foot as the offered hand.*

2. *As your partner moves behind you, raise the grabbed hand and offer the other hand palm up.*

3. *As your partner grabs your second hand, step back with your left leg. Now you are face to face with your partner.*

Classtime Conversation

"Everything that happens to you doesn't always happen in front of you: things happen behind you too. If something happens behind you, you move so that you can be face-to-face with what is happening. You need to know what or who is behind you. Then you can take care of yourself. It's easier to tie your uniform belt in front of you than it is behind you. Let's everybody try. See, it is easier in front. It's the same if someone comes up to you from behind. You need to move yourself around face-to-face so that you can clearly see your partner. Once you can see this, it is easier to move to take care of yourself."

Teaching Point

At first start teaching behind-the-back techniques with one partner standing static behind the other holding their wrists. Later, you can add motion to the technique, in which the partners approach each other from the front and one swings behind the other to grab from behind.

5. Continue to lead your partner around in a large circle.

4. Your partner lets go of the top hand. Turn back to back, reaching over and grabbing your partner's wrist.

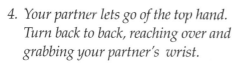

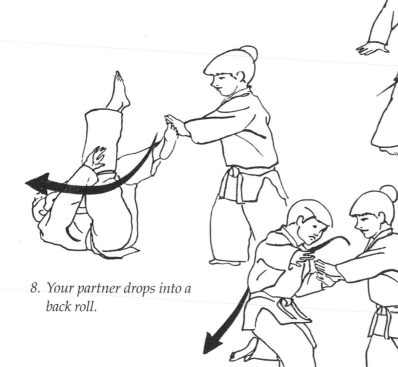

6. Gently twist your partner's wrist.

8. Your partner drops into a back roll.

7. Your partner tucks the same leg as the hand that's being twisted.

Ushiro ryotekubitori — shihonage (irimi)
Entering four-way throw from both hands grabbed from behind (front)

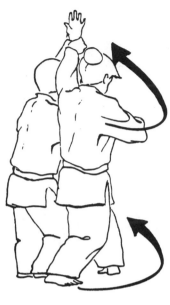

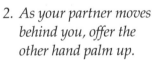

3. *As your partner grabs your second hand, step back with your other leg and turn.*

2. *As your partner moves behind you, offer the other hand palm up.*

1. *As your partner moves toward you, offer your palm up and slide forward with the same foot as the offered hand.*

Classtime Conversation
"As your partner moves to go behind you, you move around till you are face to face. Then the technique is the same, you already know shihonage, right? Now you can do it if your partner comes from the front or from behind."

Teaching Point
The technique looks different, but basically the only part of the technique that is different is the partner's approach. If you make this clear, they will be able to see that the rest of the movement is the same as doing shihonage starting-face-to-face. Break the technique into parts explaining: "From this point to this point is new, then after that it is the same as we have practiced before." Sometimes it is helpful to practice only the approach from behind and how to move to a facing position. Then add the rest of the technique.

4. Now you are face-to-face.
   Grab your partner's wrist.

5. With your outside foot, slide
   across the front of your
   partner.

6. Slide all the way under
   your partner's arm and
   pivot.

7. Your partner tucks the same
   foot as the arm being held.

8. Your partner drops into a back
   roll. As your partner falls, let go
   of your partner's arm.

Ushiro ryotekubitori — iriminage
Body throw from both hands grabbed from behind

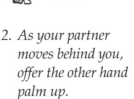

2. *As your partner
moves behind you,
offer the other hand
palm up.*

3. *As your partner grabs
your second hand, step
back with your other leg
and turn.*

1. *As your partner moves toward you,
offer your palm up and slide forward
with the same foot as the offered hand.*

Classtime Conversation

"Your partner moves around behind you, then you move around until you are facing him, then together you go around again. Looks like a dance, doesn't it? If it is your turn to approach your partner, going behind your partner, pretend like you are skiing. When your partner brings you around, you move around with them. If your partner goes down, you go down too, and up together, like you were skiing down a mountain making smooth turns. Try to blend your movements with your partner's movements."

Teaching Points

One way to get the children to move smoothly is to sing or hum while you are demonstrating the motion. They will naturally pick up a sense of rhythm to your movements as well as the happy feeling associated with music. The dojo is a place for emotional education and growth. One purpose is to develop balanced children with smiling faces, not turn out kids with vicious scowls. As instructor, it is important to maintain your authority and position as Sensei, but once in a while I act a little silly and make a mistake on purpose. The children will giggle and correct me. This is a friendlier approach that I believe is easier for the children to follow.

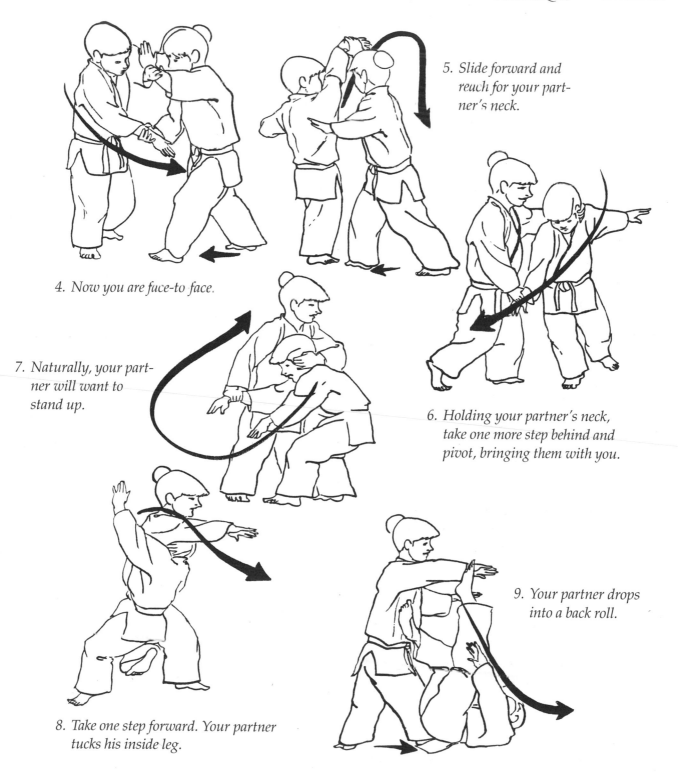

4. *Now you are face-to face.*

5. *Slide forward and reach for your partner's neck.*

6. *Holding your partner's neck, take one more step behind and pivot, bringing them with you.*

7. *Naturally, your partner will want to stand up.*

8. *Take one step forward. Your partner tucks his inside leg.*

9. *Your partner drops into a back roll.*

PART 3

CHILDREN'S TRAINING
EXERCISES AND GAMES

INTRODUCTION

The training children receive naturally when playing, hiking, or swimming is important for their growth and development. The United States is vast and blessed with wondrous natural playgrounds where children can learn and grow.

In today's world, however, access to these resources is often restricted. Urban families, for example, are forced to keep certain recreational areas off-limits to children for safety reasons. Lifestyles and recreational activities for today's children have themselves changed. Outdoor play has been replaced by video games. Over the past decades modern conveniences have reduced our daily physical exertion and exercise. The children of farmers, for example, used to rise before school to do daily chores that are now accomplished by machinery. Not so long ago children in towns and cities walked to school with their neighborhood pals. Children today, due to crime or distance, are driven to school in buses or chauffeured by their parents. Aikido, indeed any regular exercise program, can help the practitioner achieve a natural level of physical well-being higher than our current lifestyles promote.

The training games and exercises explained in this chapter are not for children only. We frequently use them in adult classes as well, especially as warm-up exercises during the cold winter months. The names for each training game and exercise were made up by the children themselves. This has resulted in a variety of unique titles that children enjoy. These training games and exercises not only build muscle, but also develop flexibility and agility. They are useful as good fun, breaking up the routine of regular class-time activities.

The most important consideration for children's playtime is, of course, safety. None of these exercises are either difficult or over-taxing. Individually, each child can decide to stop anytime. The games and exercises themselves are safe exercises, but children can easily overdo it not knowing their own limits. This can put both them and their partners at risk. It is very important that these training games and exercises be done under the direction of an instructor. Instructors need to watch carefully for hyperactive or overly excited behavior. Sometime taking an overly excited child out of an exercise and making the child watch for a while can avoid problems. Make sure the children completely understand the commands *"hajime"* (begin) and *"yame"* (stop) before you begin training.

The following pages present game and exercises for individuals, pairs, and groups. They differ greatly from the exercise one gets in a gym with man-made machines (which always reminds me of a hamster running on a wheel), in that we focus on the aspect of play. Several of the individual training exercises — such as the crab, the rabbit, and the seal — can be run as races. Students have enjoyed these training games for many years: I think it's because they appeal to the child in all of us.

INDIVIDUAL TRAINING EXERCISES

Morse Code

These are basic push-up exercises done to a variety of counts. Do a series of push-ups while spelling out names or spelling out greetings like "hello;" one letter for each count. Children with underdeveloped arm strength can do the push-ups on their knees.

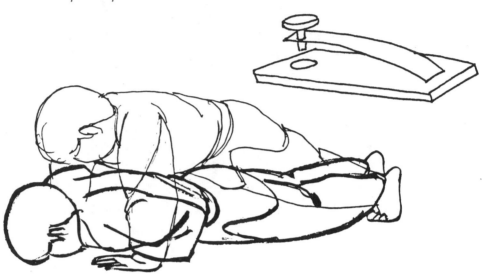

Party Blowers

With both hands locked behind the head, this sit-up exercise is done focusing on individual counting and breathing. Children lacking strength can bend both knees and touch their elbows to their knees. It is important to exhale with a loud count when you bring your body up and inhale on the way back down. This exercise is not done to the instructor's count: everyone counts in a loud voice, rotating the leader of the count, each child counting ten times. This way they count at their own pace.

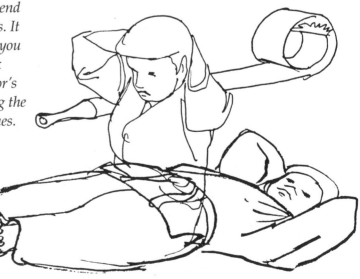

The Forklift

Start in the same position as for Party Blower. As you sit-up, raise both knees up toward your chest, touching elbows to knees, exhale, and count in a loud voice. As you lower your head and feet back down, stop a couple of inches above the mat. It is important to remember that every child has a different limit for not only this exercise but for all of them.

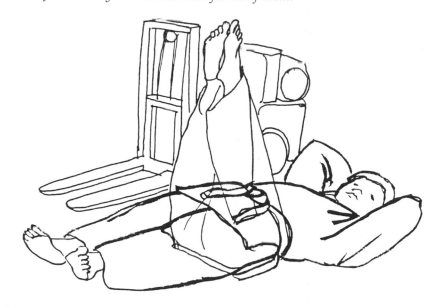

Pedaling

Rock back onto your shoulders and support your weight with your hands on your hips. With your legs in the air, move your feet in a pedaling motion, counting in a loud voice (and exhaling) each time you kick your foot forward. Everyone counts to thirty.

The Duck

Take care to do stretch exercises for knees and ankles before doing this exercise. Tuck both hands behind your back (palms out, elbows as close together as possible). Squat down as low as you can and "wad-dle" walk. Do not do this exercise for too long.

The Frog

Place both hands and both feet on the floor and jump straight up and down, then side to side, then mix the two, jumping straight up, then side, then up, etc.

The Rabbit

As in the Duck, make sure you do warm-up stretching exercises for the knees and ankles before you proceed with this exercise. Clasp both hands behind your back, and squat down as low as you can then "hop" up as high as you can and then back down to a low squatting position. Sometimes children hop without returning to a low squatting position, actually barely bending their knees. This exercise will help children to learn to use their lower limbs as a cushion.

The Crab

From a sitting position, the children put their hands behind them on the mat, plant their feet in front, and lift their hips off the mat. They can move in any direction, scurrying like crabs. Make sure that the sleeves on the childrens' uniforms aren't too long or they'll slide down and get tangled.

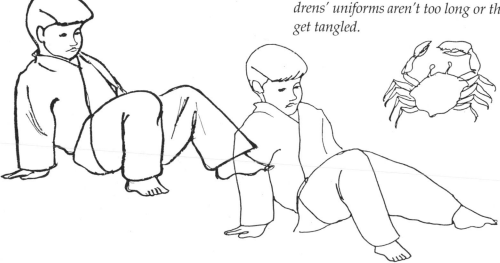

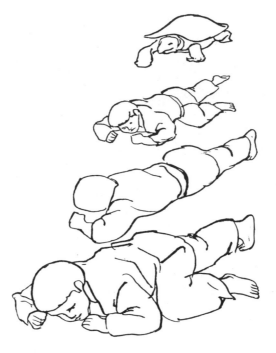

The Turtle

This is not crawling. The children lie stomach-down on the mat with fists tucked up under their shoulders. Keeping low to the mat, they move forward by alternating their elbows and knees in tandem.

The Worm

Lying on one side, scoot your hips up and draw your knees to your chest, roll to the other side, stretch out, scoot your hips and draw your knees to your chest again. At the same time, extend your arms and then bring them into your chest in a motion similar to the legs. Keep turning and repeating the motion to move forward. The easiest way to teach this exercise is to have everyone line up at one end of the mat with an instructor in front and move forward together.

The Seal

Lying flat on your stomach, raise up on struight arms, hands pointed out. Then use your upper body to move forward, while dragging your legs behind like flippers. Sometimes children try to get up on their knees: correct this, make sure their legs are outstretched behind them.

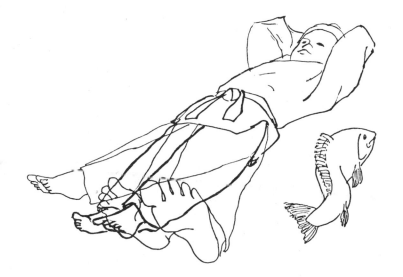

The Fish

Lying on your back with your feet together, clasp your hands behind your head, raise your head, shoulders and feet a few inches off the mat and shake quickly from side to side. This exercise helps develop stomach muscles. To keep them going, encourage the children to look at their navels while their head and feet are in the air.

Monkey Grab

This exercise is designed to improve hand grip strength. Standing, hold your arms straight out in front of you. Open and close your fists about thirty times. You can also raise your arms above your head and repeat. When children get tired they tend to hunch their shoulders forward, hunching their backs. Encourage them to keep their backs straight and count with loud voices.

The Kangaroo

From a standing position, jump forward with feet together. Mixing this jumping movement with hopping on one foot and skipping, circle around the edge of the mat.

TRAINING EXERCISES WITH A PARTNER

The Flamingo

Partners stand facing one another. Each child stands on one leg, holding one foot by the ankle behind his back. With the other hand, he pushes his partner while standing on one leg. The first child to let go of his or her ankle or fall, loses. Grabbing uniforms or pushing in the face is not allowed.

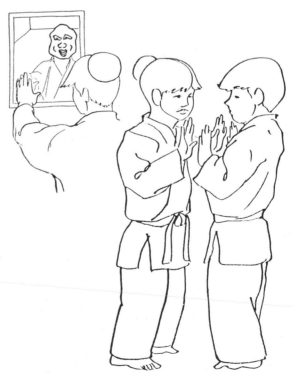

The Mirror Ghost

Partners stand with their feet close together, facing each other about one foot apart. Using only the palms of your hands, push your partner's palms in an attempt to knock them off balance. Try to use off-timing and feints to make your partner move. The one who takes a step forward or backward loses.

Meeting on the Bridge

Both partners stand face-to-face in wide stances with the same foot forward. Once in this position, the children are not allowed to move their feet. Partners push on each other's hands and forward legs to try to knock each other off balance. The partner who moves his feet first loses. Grabbing hands or uniforms is not allowed.

The Wheelbarrow

Have the children make partners with someone about the same size. As an exception to the rule, this time only, have the partner whose turn it is to be the wheelbarrow roll up their sleeves. The partner manning the wheelbarrow should not push, just hold their partner's knees or ankles and follow behind at their partner's pace.

The Baby Crab

Have the children make partners with someone about the same size. Make sure the child riding on the back jumps on high, wrapping their legs around their partner above the hips. There is no need to hurry, going too fast can make you fall down.

The Horse Jump

The child who is the "hurdle" stands with feet together, knees bent, hands in front resting on their thighs, and head tucked forward. The partner runs up from behind, places his hands on the hurdle's back and vaults over. Be sure to warn the children about behaving during this exercise. If the hurdle ducks, stands up quickly, or turns around to watch the approaching partner he could get kicked in the face. After the first child jumps over the hurdle, they change position, working their way forward around the edge of the mat area. This exercise can be done with large groups and multiple hurdles.

Over the Line

Using two uniform belts, form parallel boundary lines about six feet apart. Partners stand back to back between the lines and lock arms behind them. The object is to push one's partner over the line. If both children fall down inside the lines it is a draw.

The See-Saw

Partners stand back-to-back and lock arms behind them. One partner bends their knees and lifts their partner onto their back. The partner being lifted lifts both legs straight up into the air, feet together, being careful not to over-balance. To change partners, the child doing the lifting should have his or her arms wrapped from the inside of their partner's arms. This game-exercise should be done carefully and slowly to avoid having the children flipping over the heads of their partners.

The Mad Rabbit

Face your partner, both in a squatting position, arms crossed in front of your chest. Hop toward one another and push into each other without losing your balance. The first partner to fall backward or forward onto his or her hip or knees or whose arms come uncrossed loses. Make sure you tell the children to keep looking at their partner's face, not to look down at the mat. This will help keep them from bumping heads.

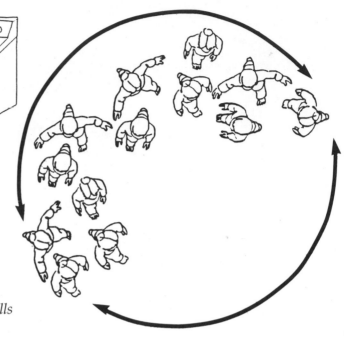

GROUP TRAINING GAMES

Washing Machine

Have the children jog easily around the edge of the mat in the same direction. The instructor calls out a signal to change direction. Vary the time intervals between signal changes. For example, two short intervals followed by a long interval and then three more short intervals. This training game works on developing the ability to respond physically to audio stimulus.

The Crosswalk

Separate the children into four groups, one in each corner of the mat. All at the same time have each group jog lightly to their opposite corner and back a few times. The object is to not collide with any of the other children as each group crosses the mat, helping to improve concentration and coordination.

The Ninja

Line the children up around the walls of the dojo. The instructor calls out a signal to begin walking sideways, pressed up against the wall. Call out another signal to change directions, varying the time intervals in between.

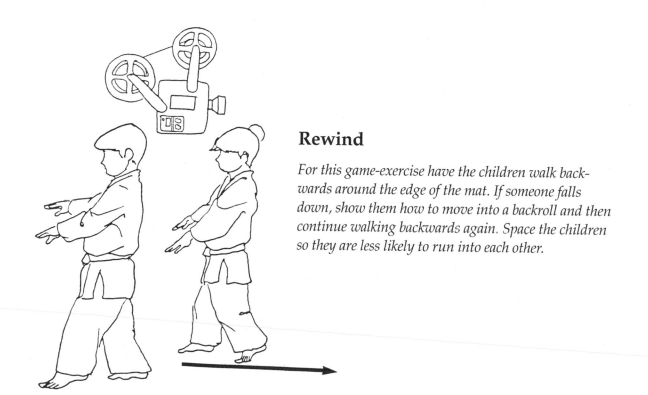

Rewind

For this game-exercise have the children walk backwards around the edge of the mat. If someone falls down, show them how to move into a backroll and then continue walking backwards again. Space the children so they are less likely to run into each other.

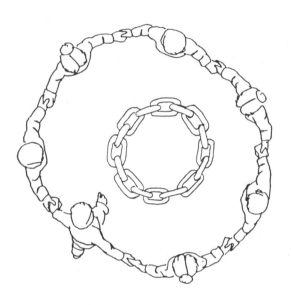

The Circle Chain

Have all the children form a circle facing into the circle. Feet should be about shoulder width apart. About ten children to a circle is a good number. Everyone holds their partner's wrists on each side of them, forming a chain. As everyone pulls and pushes (without letting go), the first to step forward or backward must leave the circle. Continue the game until only two are left. Their contest will determine the winner.

The Caterpillar

In groups of five or six, have the children stand back to back and lock elbows. At the instructors signal, everyone begins pushing backwards toward the center starting the "caterpillar" to move. If there are more than one group, they can push against each other. If any child falls down or the whole group falls down, the instructor must stop the game immediately and start again. Continue the exercise in three-minute periods followed by a rest.

The Super Horse Jump

This is the same as the horse jump game with a partner, only for larger groups. Children line up about six to eight feet apart around the edge of the mat facing in the same direction. As a child jumps over their last hurdle. they become the next hurdle until everyone has had at least one turn. As instructor, watch when small children attempt jumping over taller children. Instruct the taller ones to bend down as low as they can.

The Secret Roll

This game-exercise is for practicing rolls and developing eye-body movement coordination. As instructor, work out a set of physical signals which signal the direction to roll in. When the children see the signs, they must roll in the proper direction. It depends on the size of the dojo, but you should probably have only two or three children, spaced widely apart, rolling at the same time. As the other children wait their turn they can act as judges to see if those rolling move correctly. This exercise of seeing, confirming, and reacting to visual stimulus is basic self-defense.

Front roll.

Back roll.

Front roll (to the side).

Back roll (to the side).

Word Signal

This game-exercise is for practicing rolls and developing audio-body movement coordination. Work up a set of passwords which signal the direction to roll in. When the children hear the passwords they must match the password with the correct roll. Colors, animals, street names or simple Japanese words can be used, for example. This exercise trains the children to respond consciously with physical motion to audio stimulus. As in the Secret Roll game, have only two or three children roll at the same time to avoid collisions. If a child makes a mistake or gets stuck and can't move, ask the other children observing as judges to help point out the correct way. This will also help hold their attention while they wait their turn.

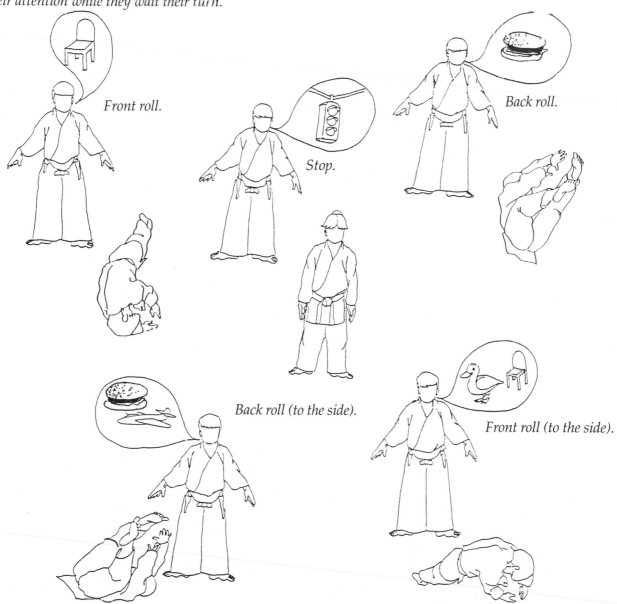

Front roll.

Stop.

Back roll.

Back roll (to the side).

Front roll (to the side).

GAMES AND EXERCISES USING BOKKENS, JOS, AND UNIFORM BELTS

Jumping Bokken

Line up a number of bokkens parallel to one another, spaced at different distances apart. As the instructor calls out a number, the children must respond by jumping over the same number of bokkens with both feet. It is best to use bokkens or old keiko-gi belts for this game-exercise. If you use jos and someone steps on them they might slip, because the jos are round and will roll. You can also have the children do this on one leg to increase the difficulty.

Over and Under

Divide the children into two groups. The first group forms a line, with the children spaced about six feet apart. In a kneeling position, have the children hold a jo, by one end in each hand, one held high, the other held low. Smaller children can hold only one jo, either low or high. The older children can hold two. It is good training for strengthening arm muscles and hand grip. Do not have two children hold both ends of the jo between them, even if they complain that they are too heavy. This can be dangerous because the jo is too rigidly held in place. One at a time the second group goes through, jumping over or ducking under each jo as they pass by. Bokken can be used for this exercise as well.

Aihanmi Katate Jo Taoshi
Same hand grab, push-pull with the jo

Both partners face each other standing with the same foot forward. With the same hand as the forward foot each of them holds one end of the jo. At the instructor's signal, both push, pull or feint to knock their partner off balance. The one who falls over, takes a step, or loses his or her grip on the jo loses.

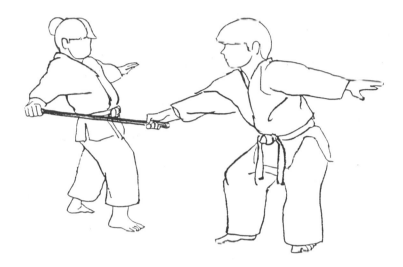

Ryote Jo Taoshi
Both hand grab, push-pull with the jo

Partners stand facing each other squarely with their feet about shoulder width apart. Holding two jos by the ends between them, one in each hand, both partners push, pull, and feint to knock their partner off balance. The first to fall down, take a step, or let go of the jo loses.

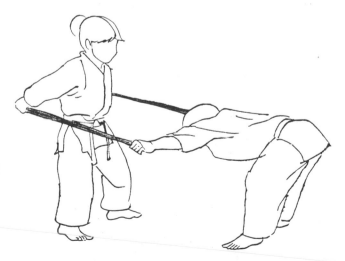

Tug o' War

Mark a center line with an old uniform belt. Have partners stand one on each side of the line holding onto the ends of another belt with both hands. The object of the game is to pull your partner until he or she steps over the center line. The one to step over the line, fall down, or let go of the belt loses. One purpose of this exercise is to strengthen hand grip, so don't let the children wrap the belt around their hands. You can do this exercise from a squatting position as well.

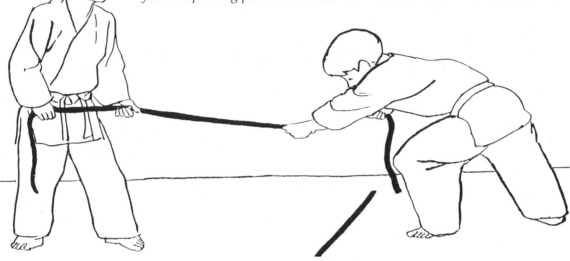

Ryote Obi Taoshi
A belt in each hand tug o' war

With a belt held near the end in each hand, partners stand facing each other about the distance apart as the length of the belts. Standing with feet about shoulder-width apart, partners push, pull and feint, to try to take their partner's balance. The one to let go of the belt, fall down or take a step loses. Do not wrap the belt around your hand. It is better grip training to hold the belt in your hand and you can easily let go if you fall down.

Aihanmi Obi Taoshi

Same hand grab belt tug o' war

With the same foot forward, feet shoulder-width apart, partners face each other with the length of a uniform belt between them. Holding the belt near the end with the same hand as the forward foot, partners push, pull, or feint to try to take their partner's balance. The one to let go of the belt, fall down, or take a step loses. Do not wrap the belt around your hand. It is better grip training to hold the belt in your hand; you can easily let go if you fall down.

ABOUT THE AUTHOR

Gaku Homma is founder and chief instructor of Aikido Nippon Kan in Denver, Colorado U.S.A. He has practiced under Morehei Ueshiba, the founder of Aikido, as well as other high-ranking Aikido instructors. As an independent instructor, he has delighted thousands of students with his dynamic style of Aikido. Gaku Homma has dedicated his practice of Aikido to blending traditional Japanese culture with the contemporary world. In addition to *Children and the Martial Arts: An Aikido Point of View,* he has written *Aikido for Life.*

ABOUT THE ILLUSTRATOR

Daniel Marion, Jr. received his Bachelor's Degree in Art and Education from the University of Wisconsin-Milwaukee, where he also studied Judo. After serving as a photographer for the Army for two years, he embarked on an art teaching career in Milwaukee. He is currently an art teacher at Hutchinson Elementary School and a doctoral student in multicultural education. He lives in Denver, Colorado and is a third degree black belt at Nippon Kan.